The junior church programme with a difference!

Three + One
Festivals One

Michael Forster

Kevin Mayhew

First published in 2000 by
KEVIN MAYHEW LTD
Buxhall
Stowmarket
Suffolk IP14 3BW

0 1 2 3 4 5 6 7 8 9

ISBN 1 84003 641 9
Catalogue No 1500389

Cover design by Jonathan Stroulger
Illustrated by Simon Smith
Edited by Katherine Laidler
Typesetting by Louise Selfe
Printed in Great Britain

Contents

This series of books is dedicated to the worshippers of all ages at my own church in Anstey, Leicestershire, with gratitude for their openness and enthusiasm in field-testing and developing this concept.

Special thanks are due to Laura Doody and Claire Pearson for their help with the proof-reading.

Foreword

Welcome to the Festivals edition of *Three + One*! This is designed to complement the standard volumes, which are intended for use throughout the year, with material specifically designed to focus upon the main festivals, Christmas, Easter and Pentecost. Another volume provides for Harvest Festival, Church Anniversary and Remembrance Sunday.

As you will know if you have used the standard volumes, the emphasis in this programme is placed upon building relationships, including the children in something they may come to value, telling the faith story in engaging ways, and letting the 'learning' be a spin-off benefit. I am convinced that that is a more effective way of working with children than focusing just on the imparting of knowledge.

As with the rest of the programme, the sessions in this book are arranged in sets of four: three 'Junior Church' sessions building into an all-age service on the fourth Sunday – which in this case will be one of the festivals – when the children's work will be celebrated and valued by the whole church fellowship, and the adults will have the opportunity to learn both from and with the children.

There is just one important difference which relates to the 'ticked' activities – so it's worth revisiting the 'How to use this book' section, even if you feel you're well accustomed to the concept by now.

I hope and pray that these resources will open minds of all ages to the wonder of God's love and the joy of sharing it, rather than merely fill them up with doctrines and ethical propositions.

All that will follow. The first thing – and the prime thing – is to *relate*.

Enjoy the book. Enjoy one another. Oh, and enjoy God, of course!

MICHAEL FORSTER

Introduction

This series of books arose out of a particular need. We were finding the usual age-based 'classes' difficult to sustain in our context, and mixed-age groups seemed the only option – but the cry went up, 'You can't teach five- and ten-year-olds in the same class' (I'll have more to say about the 'teaching' idea later).

At the same time, we wanted to include the children much more in the actual planning of our monthly all-age worship which, until then, tended to be a bit of a one-man show that was done *for* rather than *with* them. But just when do you gather increasingly busy and pressurised children together to plan services?

This is what we decided to do. We would take an overall theme that could be presented in three weekly stories, and the learning process would consist of fun activities: story-telling, art and craft, drama, music, some of which could then become the basis for the all-age service. But what if some children could only come for two of the weeks? Would they be left out? Clearly, each week's story, while relating to the three-week theme, would need to be able to stand alone.

Wouldn't it make the all-age worship terribly long and overladen with material? Probably, if *all* the previous three-weeks' work were used – so the Junior Church would choose just one of the three stories as the focus for the service, but let the worship leader put it into context with the help of the pictures, models, etc., that the children had made. That would enable most of the art and craftwork to be on display in the church, providing a visual background to the storytelling. And storytelling really is the basis of communicating our faith. Ask any of our Jewish cousins! Or ask Jesus!

So this material was written, and some of it has been used, and the basic idea and format have been tried and tested. One exciting result has been the releasing of some previously unrecognised creativity as children who had not been in the limelight before took the basic ideas and developed them in wonderfully imaginative ways. In the very first month of using this material, we discovered some real hidden treasure – and we did so in worship where we could properly celebrate and give thanks for it.

And that brings me to the most important thing we learned from this. Don't let the all-age worship become a talking shop! The discussion-type activities will quickly lose their appeal if that happens. We saw this coming in good time and proposed the setting up of a Worship and Mission Action Group (definitely *not* a committee) within the church to carry forward some of the ideas that come out of these sessions. Such a group must be a 'ginger group' rather than a management committee. They should not get bogged down in the minutiae of keeping new projects going, but simply research ideas and present possibilities to the relevant meetings (more than once if necessary!) to ensure that they are not simply lost in a sea of good intentions. If that were to happen – if the cards, etc., that the discussion groups produce were simply thrown away or filed and forgotten, we think it would not be long before the worship became stale: 'Oh, another of those silly discussions, again.' However, if the action group is set up, and enabled to work well, the all-age worship could become a real source of inspiration for the Church's mission – something through which the Holy Spirit might breathe renewal into the Church and the local community.

How to get the best from this book

The book is based on three 'units', each of which is a four-week cycle: three Junior Church sessions, and one all-age service. Clearly, you will need to plan so that the 'fourth' Sunday in each unit falls on the relevant festival. You will also, of course, need to plan how this fits into the year as a whole. In field-testing this idea, we actually took a little time to plan the year's outline. After that, it was a very simple matter to follow the system through.

As with the other volumes in this series, each session divides into a number of activities, and a worksheet is also provided either to do in the session or as a take-home resource. There will almost certainly be too much here for the single session of perhaps 45 minutes that most Junior Churches have – so *don't think you have to use it all*. (Nothing destroys a good learning environment like trying to cram too much in!) Choose what you think best fits your group in each particular case, and perhaps have other items standing by in case you run out. Much, of course, will depend on the number of children you have. A small Junior Church could work all together, whereas a large one might start together for the storytelling and then break up into several multi-age groups, each focusing on a different activity – some children producing art and craft work, others doing drama, learning new songs, etc. The important thing to remember is that the all-age worship in Week 4 should be a celebration of whatever has been done – not a goal to be striven for and which becomes a blight on the sessions because the children are under pressure.

Most importantly of all, remember the central aims. The session should:

- be enjoyable for all concerned
- make all the children feel valued and cared about
- contribute to building relationships

If you do these things, then the 'teaching' will happen, because children are great learners if the environment is right. They'll virtually teach themselves!

Let's have a look at each of the elements that comprise the sessions.

Thinking about it

This is vital – the advance preparation need not be unduly time-consuming or tedious, but it will transform the actual session. In fact, we found that the preparation required in using this material was much less onerous than preparing traditional lessons.

- An advance meeting of key people would be a good idea, when you can take an overview of the unit and ensure that the necessary resources are available.

- Then each week look through the relevant session thoroughly and give some thought to which would be the most appropriate and helpful elements to concentrate on, in your situation.

- Prepare any resources: art/craft materials, visual aids, legitimate photo-copies, etc., that you need. Try to anticipate the kinds of questions the children might ask – or that you could helpfully ask them.

What's the point?

It's helpful to have a specific point in mind that we wish to convey. This does not mean we can't find other things in the text, but one point retained is better than five confused or forgotten – and more likely to engage the children's attention, too! They have the rest of their lives to explore the countless layers of meaning, so don't let's spoil it by cramming them too full of rich food!

Now for the session itself.

Doing it

Prayer

An opening prayer is offered for those who wish to use it. However, we should be careful about stereotyping prayer too much as merely 'talking to God'. It might be worth thinking about encouraging children to think of prayer as consciously *being* with God – sometimes quietly, but also in the more active parts of life. So let God join in the activities, the fun, most of all in the growing relationships between staff, parents and children. In a different kind of way, the whole session is 'prayer' – and both kinds are important.

For this reason, the prayers are short and are all focused in such a way as to point the children to that greater reality.

From the known to the unknown

Jesus understood well the first principle of teaching: begin with what people know, and only then introduce the new. His most effective teaching, according to the Gospel records, was in parables. Often, he simply didn't mention scripture at all.

That is not an argument against biblical teaching – rather it is a plea to make it more effective. Children are wonderful at making connections – much better than we adults with our 'disciplined' (trammelled?) minds. So we begin by appealing to what they know, and *then* tell them the biblical story. With little or no prompting, they often will then grasp joyfully and spontaneously for themselves what we so often labour painfully and ineffectually to drill into them – and no one is more guilty of that than I am!

Tell the story

Storytelling is the basis of keeping the faith alive. Our Jewish forebears kept their children in the faith by telling and retelling vibrant stories, often around meal-tables, camp fires or in other informal settings, with plenty of song and laughter to help it along. So a child-friendly version of a Bible story is the mainstay of each week's material. It's a good idea to read it a few times in advance, so you are familiar and can half-tell, half-read it to the children with plenty of eye contact and other interaction. Or you can get them to tell it to each other by acting it out – see 'Drama', below. You may also find it useful to have some visual aids handy, or think of some questions you can ask, breaking off from the narrative whenever you choose to ask, 'How do you think God felt about that?' 'What d'you think happened then?' 'What would you have done about that?' etc. This will all help to maintain the children's interest – with a little imagination you can easily keep them enthralled!

Respond to the story

The children's response to the story now forms the basis of the rest of the session. It's important that they're encouraged to be spontaneous and really engage with the characters and the action. Here you will want to focus on the forms of response that are best suited to your situation, but the first one, 'Discussion', should never be missed out.

Discussion

Keep it lively, informal, chatty – and don't let any child feel silly or wrong, whatever they say or ask. The important thing is that they grow by being able to interact freely with the text. You may want to feed in some of their questions or reactions to the storytelling in the all age worship. Most importantly, don't be anxious about this section – and don't let the discussion become either too long or too heavy! Just enjoy a bit of a chat with the children.

Song

Some songs are suggested. Either revisiting well-known ones or learning new ones can be fun, and perhaps sometimes the children can teach some of the new ones to the adults in the all-age worship. However, be careful not to let the Junior Church session degenerate into mere rehearsal. Let them have fun singing the songs, confident that even imperfectly sung they will still form acceptable worship. If some of the children have instruments, there's no reason why they couldn't be used at this time. All the songs recommended in these pages can be found in one or more of the following Kevin Mayhew publications (among others):

- *Kidsource*
- *The Source*
- *The Children's Hymn Book*
- *21st Century Folk Hymnal*

Art and craft

This will probably form quite a big part of the session: children of all ages and abilities can work together to produce models, drawings, paintings, etc. A few ideas are suggested, but they don't need to be limited. This was the area where we found children really showed their ingenuity and made immensely valuable contributions, producing and effecting ideas that would never have occurred to us!

✔ The 'ticked' activity only occurs in Week 3 – there isn't a choice since, clearly, you will want to focus on the story that relates most closely to the festival concerned. For example, on Easter Sunday, you will want to focus on the resurrection, not on the Red Sea or Gethsemane. As before, though, what is important in the 'ticked' activities, is that the children know *why* they are preparing these things – a few simple words of explanation will help them to relate it to the story they have heard and the point you were trying to make.

In terms of drawing and painting, the options are limited only by the size of the group and the children's imaginations! They could build up over the three weeks a complete 'strip cartoon' of the whole story, to be used in introducing the theme in all-age worship. The pictures could be on a continuous frieze, or on cardboard placards held on poles by the children, or separate pictures fixed around the walls before the service starts. Children could enter at different points as the story's told, holding their placard, or – well, you think of your own ideas – they'll probably be better than mine, anyway.

Drama

A dramatised version of the story is included. It can simply be used as a dramatised reading, with different children literally reading the parts, or it could be developed, if your group has a flair for it, into something much bigger. Adapt it freely to suit your group. If you need more parts, try splitting the narrator's part between several children, or add in one or two new characters. During the free discussion of the story things might emerge that it would be good to include in the dialogue. Feel free to photocopy these pages and make your own alterations if you wish. The drama can then either be used simply as a teaching aid or rehearsed and presented in the all-age worship. An added touch might be to use a domestic tape recorder to record it – then each child could take home a recording of a play with their own voice on it!

Worksheet

This is included for you to use as you see fit. You could have some of the children colour in the pictures and display them at the service, or you could let a group work through the sheet as part of the session; or it could simply be given to them as a take-home sheet to help them remember the session and/or to share with their families.

All-age worship

This is the culmination of the unit, but please don't allow preparation for it to dominate and spoil the sessions. It's not a performance, and no one will mind if what the children produce isn't beautifully polished – the main thing is that they should be seen to be enjoying it.

The services are designed to be truly 'all age', involving the whole congregation, and – most importantly – giving opportunities for interaction across the age groups. There are no 'children's talks', but rather all-age activities.

This approach needs to be reflected in the overall balance of the service, so that it is one in which all people can participate rather than a children's service with the adults as indulgent spectators.

Let's take a look at the various elements:

Songs

Naturally, there will be songs specifically chosen by the children, or at least with them in mind. But including some more 'adult' hymns not only shows respect to the older worshippers but also requires the children to sample a more varied diet and hopefully broaden their taste.

Welcome and statement of the theme

An example is given, but please feel free to use your own words and adapt it for your own circumstances. It's an important element in the service, for it introduces the chosen theme and sets it in the wider context. It is also a jolly good opportunity to point out some of the creative work the children have done, and have it suitably acknowledged by the congregation.

Prayers

Again, an opening prayer is offered, but it's not mandatory! Local worship leaders will probably want to do something more appropriate to the particular setting.

Word and action

The Bible story from Week 3 is not only read but reinforced with an all-age activity. The essential point is to make this at once meaningful and enjoyable. If people enjoy it, they're far more likely to enter into it. One important point, though: you know your own congregation best, and are in a position to ensure that people aren't treated insensitively. If you know that Mrs X doesn't like being in the limelight, then avoid drawing attention to her.

There is one very important general point, which we learned in the field testing. Where this part of the worship involves discussing ideas, don't let it become a mere talking shop! The discussion-type activities will quickly lose their appeal if that happens. We saw this coming in good time and proposed the setting up of a Worship and Mission Action Group (definitely *not* a committee) within the church to carry forward some of the ideas that come out of these sessions. Such a group must be a 'ginger group' rather than a management committee. They should not get bogged down in the minutiae of keeping new projects going, but simply research ideas and present possibilities to the relevant meetings (more than once if necessary!) to ensure that they are not simply lost in a sea of good intentions. If that were to happen – if the ideas that arose from this section were simply filed and forgotten – we think it would not be long before the worship became stale:

'Oh, another of those silly discussions, again'. However, if the action group is set up, and enabled to work well, the all-age worship could become a real source of inspiration for the church's mission – something through which the Holy Spirit might breathe renewal into the church and the local community.

Finally, watch the time. People will warm to the subject and be difficult to stop! You will also then be deluged with responses, many of them duplicated in different groups. Keep the discussion short and to the point, and move on.

Offertory prayer

All we do and give is a free response to what God does for and gives to us. The offertory prayer is a good opportunity to highlight that point. This helps to avoid religion becoming 'works centred' rather than being a free, joyful response to God's grace.

Reading

Because you're using imaginatively rewritten stories, it's very important to read from a standard Bible in the service, and this point should never be overlooked. Children – and especially the older ones and the young people – need to hear the Bible read and come to appreciate it for themselves.

Talk

It's marked 'optional', but it's actually quite an important part of the service. As with the Bible, the traditional sermon is too valuable (when done well) to throw away. In a service of this nature, a short talk helps develop and maintain the skills of listening and reasoning. Keep it short, though, or it will have the opposite effect! On the other hand, if the service is running over time, this is an element that could *occasionally* be omitted.

Notices and family news

All too often, notices are regarded as an intrusion, and ways are often found to 'get them out of the way'. But surely, this is the life of the church that is being shared here – and should it not be offered to God, along with the lives of his people? In the service order here, I've suggested putting the notices directly before the intercessions, so they can then feed into the prayers, thus integrating them more closely into the worship.

This is also a suitable time to do something else – the 'Family news'. People who have, for example, a birthday, or a wedding anniversary, or perhaps who are changing jobs, retiring or whatever, can share that with the congregation. A supply of cards can be kept in the church, with a suitably general message in them, to be handed out to people along with the good wishes and applause of the congregation. This is one slot we daren't leave out at Anstey, or we hear about it!

Intercessions

If Jesus was 'the man for others' it's hard to imagine worship that is genuinely Christian and doesn't include some sort of intercession for others. You will certainly want to include some of the children's own concerns that have emerged in the sessions in these prayers. You might also want to use some of the artwork to help the congregation focus on particular things. Whoever leads these, try to ensure that they are done thoughtfully, with a concern for the whole of God's creation, and not just Christians.

Closing prayer/benediction

Another element that should be kept short but meaningful! This is where the congregation are sent out into the world to live in some way the values and ideals they have expressed in their worship.

Now, go to it!

Most importantly of all – use the material imaginatively; make it work *for you*. It is your servant, not your director. What matters is that all involved enjoy the sessions, learn about valuing and being valued, build relationships with each other and with 'staff', and learn along the way.

That's how Jesus worked whenever he could. And it's not a bad example to follow!

Unit 1
Countdown to Christmas

Overview of the unit

Theme: God is here in the unexpected

As is his way, God breaks with all social norms and conventions when he chooses whom he will involve in the great event of the Incarnation. The apparently important people are sidelined while those whom, for one reason or another, the world counts worthless are given vital roles to play.

We take three key events:

Week 1: Zechariah and Elizabeth – unexpected parents

Elizabeth, who is generally considered to be under some sort of punishment since she has no children, is chosen to be the mother of John the Baptist, the one who will prepare the way for Jesus. Meanwhile, her husband, a priest, is struck dumb for lack of faith.

Week 2: Mary – unexpected Mother

Mary, for quite a different reason, is also unable to have children – and is therefore a woman of no importance in society's eyes. In order to fulfil her role in life she will need the help of someone with the power to create life. But it won't be Joseph.

Week 3: Shepherds – unexpected guests

The great event happens, but has God made a mistake – or a statement? Neither the setting nor the invited guests make a very impressive sight by any standards the world recognises.

Christmas all-age worship

This will focus on the Christmas story – not the story of Zechariah or the Annunciation – so the theme of the service will come from Week 3, emphasised in the 'Word and action' material, but some of the art and craft work the children have done in the other weeks will be used to decorate the church and set the wider context of the story.

Week 1: Zechariah and Elizabeth – unexpected parents

Thinking about it

What's the point?

God's ways are not our ways: in particular, our way of deciding who is important is not God's way. Right from the beginning of the Gospel, Luke shows us a God who gives pride of place to those who are pushed aside by society. It was Zechariah who seemed to have the important (and successful) role, while Elizabeth was not only a nobody but a failure. In giving her the central part to play in this instalment of his story, God challenges some of our basic attitudes.

Doing it

Prayer

Loving God,
thank you for showing us that we're all important to you.
Thank you for this time to be together
and share your love with one another.
Help us to enjoy it and to know that you are with us.
Amen.

From the known to the unknown

Have the children ever been surprised by someone doing better than they expected? Maybe they thought a particular person was stupid because they didn't talk very much, or thought someone didn't care because they were a bit shy, only to find out differently later. That's a bit how things were in this story. Elizabeth and Zechariah wanted children, but couldn't have them – and the silly neighbours blamed Elizabeth and thought God was punishing her for something!

Tell the story: Luke 1:5-25, 57-66

(See page 22 for a dramatised version of this story.)

A most unusual Deity

Zechariah was late for worship – which wouldn't have been quite so bad if he hadn't been leading it. He was worried about his wife, Elizabeth, who was unhappy.

'You're on duty today,' she said, sternly. 'Don't worry about me – I'm getting used to it, now.'

So, what was Elizabeth getting used to, that she was so unhappy about?

She and Zechariah didn't have any children, and as they were both getting on a bit, it looked as though they never would have.

'I wouldn't mind if people didn't gossip so much about you,' Zechariah said.

'Oh, they're just full of silly ideas,' said Elizabeth. 'I know they all blame me, and think God's punishing me for something, but you and I know better, don't we?'

Zechariah couldn't help worrying as he went into the Temple's special holy place to light the incense. He nearly jumped out of his skin when he heard a voice. 'Hi, Zack, what's new? Oh, sorry, that's what I'm here to tell you, isn't it?' Turning round, he saw the most bizarre-looking man he'd seen in his life: quite short, very round, and wearing a long brown robe tied with a girdle where his waist should have been. His head was shaven, leaving just a little ring of hair around a central bald patch, and in his hand he held what looked like a string of beads. The man raised a hand in blessing. 'Peace,' he said.

'Never mind "peace",' Zechariah retorted. 'You aren't supposed to be in here.'

'Oh, but I am,' the man beamed. 'God sent me. Gabriel's the name – the Archangel Gabriel to be formal, but Archie to my friends.'

Zechariah ignored the outstretched hand. 'Angel, my eye!' he said. 'I don't know what you *do* look like, but it's not an angel.'

The intruder stopped smiling. 'Oh, all right – I suppose I'll have to pander to the usual cliché. What is it, then – wings, halo and golden harp? Give me a second.'

Actually, it took a bit less – just 865 milliseconds, but Zechariah wasn't counting.

'Now,' sighed the stranger, 'is that better?'

Zechariah was speechless – not for the last time, as it turned out, but you'll have to wait for that bit. Gabriel took advantage of the silence. 'Right, now listen and listen good, because I don't want to be in this gear any longer than I have to. God's heard your prayers, and you're going to have a son. You're to call him John – don't ask why, just accept it, OK? Great stuff – big celebrations, and all that – joy, jubilation, you know the form – and he's going to grow up to be quite something. Like, if you think I looked a bit odd, just now – well, you ain't seen nothing yet. And yes, I do know that was a double negative, but angels are allowed to be ungrammatical because they haven't got Key Stage One in heaven. OK? Now, where was I? Oh, yes – John – he's going to be one heck of a street preacher – turn lots of people back to God, and get everyone ready for the really big event. Yes, that's it – the Messiah. (Cue trumpets and heavenly chorus – on second thoughts, we'll leave that bit for later.)'

'But we're old,' Zechariah stammered. 'How can Elizabeth and I have children, now?'

'Just who d'you think I am?' Gabriel demanded, 'a used donkey salesman? I'm Gabriel – I stand right in front of the throne of God – which beats this little padded cell of yours, I can tell you – and you're doubting me? Right –

that's it – no more Mr Nice Guy. I'm striking you dumb for lack of faith – just until the baby's born. Try explaining that to your congregation.' And he was gone.

'The congregation!' thought Zechariah. 'What am I going to tell them?' All he could do was go and make signs at them, and then go home to Elizabeth.

When the news of the pregnancy got out, everybody was thrilled to bits, and when the baby was born they threw a great party. After eight days, Zechariah and Elizabeth took him to the temple to dedicate him. 'We want to call him John,' said Elizabeth.

People were amazed. 'John? But there's no one in Zechariah's family called John. You've got to name him after someone in his father's family – it's traditional.'

Zechariah still couldn't speak, so he gestured that he wanted something to write on, and he wrote down, 'His name is John.'

Everyone thought that was very unusual – and they weren't at all sure that a good religious family should be doing unusual things. Doing unusual things certainly wasn't usual.

'Well, there you go,' Elizabeth smiled. 'Maybe God's a lot more unusual than we think.'

Respond to the story

Discussion

How do the children think Elizabeth felt when she knew she was having a baby?

- Overjoyed?
- Perhaps just a little nervous?
- Relieved that the gossips had been proved wrong?

Song

One or more of the following songs might be used here and/or in the all-age worship:

God's people aren't super-brave superheroes
I walk by faith
Nobody's a nobody
Oh! Oh! Oh! how good is the Lord
Our God is so great

Art and craft

Draw or paint a picture of Elizabeth and Zechariah celebrating John's birth.

This is the key picture, but you might want to do others in addition to it, such as:

- Zechariah in the temple, burning incense
- Zechariah making signs to his congregation
- Zechariah writing down John's name

Drama: A most unusual Deity

Narrator	Zechariah was late for worship – which wouldn't have been quite so bad if he hadn't been leading it. He was worried about his wife, Elizabeth, who was unhappy.
Elizabeth	You're on duty today. Don't worry about me – I'm getting used to it, now.
Narrator	So, what was Elizabeth getting used to, that she was so unhappy about? She and Zechariah didn't have any children, and as they were both getting on a bit, it looked as though they never would have.
Zechariah	I wouldn't mind if people didn't gossip so much about you.
Elizabeth	Oh, they're just full of silly ideas. I know they all blame me, and think God's punishing me for something, but you and I know better, don't we?
Narrator	Zechariah couldn't help worrying as he went into the Temple's special holy place to light the incense. He nearly jumped out of his skin when he heard a voice.
Gabriel	Hi, Zack, what's new? Oh, sorry, that's what I'm here to tell you, isn't it?
Narrator	Turning round, Zechariah saw the most bizarre-looking man he'd seen in his life: quite short, very round, and wearing a long brown robe tied with a girdle where his waist should have been. His head was shaven, leaving just a little ring of hair around a central bald patch, and in his hand he held what looked like a string of beads. The man raised a hand in blessing.
Gabriel	Peace.
Zechariah	Never mind 'peace'. You aren't supposed to be in here.
Gabriel	Oh, but I am. God sent me. Gabriel's the name – the Archangel Gabriel to be formal, but Archie to my friends.
Zechariah	Angel, my eye! I don't know what you *do* look like, but it's not an angel.
Gabriel	Oh, all right – I suppose I'll have to pander to the usual cliché. What is it, then – wings, halo and golden harp? Give me a second.
Narrator	Actually, it took a bit less – just 865 milliseconds, but Zechariah wasn't counting.
Gabriel	[*Sighs*] Now, is that better?
Narrator	Zechariah was speechless – not for the last time, as it turned out, but you'll have to wait for that bit. Gabriel took advantage of the silence.
Gabriel	Right, now listen and listen good, because I don't want to be in this gear any longer than I have to. God's heard your prayers, and you're going to have a son. You're to call him John – don't ask why, just believe, OK? Great stuff – big celebrations, and all that – joy, jubilation, you know the form – and he's going to

grow up to be quite something. Like, if you think I looked a bit odd, just now – well, you ain't seen nothing yet. And yes, I do know that was a double negative, but angels are allowed to be ungrammatical because we haven't got Key Stage One in heaven. OK? Now, where was I? Oh, yes – John – he's going to be one heck of a street preacher – turn lots of people back to God, and get everyone ready for the really big event. Yes, that's it – the Messiah. (Cue trumpets and heavenly chorus – on second thoughts, we'll leave that bit for later.)

Zechariah   But Elizabeth and I are old. How can we have children, now?

Gabriel   Just who d'you think I am – a used donkey salesman? I'm Gabriel – I stand right in front of the throne of God – which beats this little padded cell of yours, I can tell you – and you're doubting me? Right – that's it – no more Mr Nice Guy. From now on, I'm striking you dumb for lack of faith – just until the baby's born. Try explaining that to your congregation.

Narrator   And the Angel was gone, as suddenly as he had come.

Zechariah   The congregation! What am I going to tell them?

Narrator   All Zechariah could do was go and make signs at them, and then go home to Elizabeth. When the news of the pregnancy got out, everybody was thrilled to bits, and when the baby was born they threw a great party. After eight days, Zechariah and Elizabeth took him to the Temple to dedicate him.

Elizabeth   We want to call him John.

Narrator   People were amazed.

Friend   John? But there's no one in Zechariah's family called John. You've got to name him after someone in his father's family – it's traditional.

Narrator   Zechariah still couldn't speak, so he gestured that he wanted something to write on, and he wrote down, 'His name is John.' Everyone thought that was very unusual – and they weren't at all sure that a good religious family should be doing unusual things. Doing unusual things certainly wasn't usual.

Elizabeth   Well, there you go. Maybe God's a lot more unusual than we think.

This is what the Lord has done for me. (Luke 1:25)

Zechariah has burned so much incense he can't see the angel for the smoke! Colour the dotted shapes to find Gabriel again.

WORDSEARCH
Find the following words in the grid:

ZECHARIAH, ELIZABETH, GOSSIP, JOHN, GABRIEL, TEMPLE, INCENSE, GOD, ARCHANGEL, CHILDREN, OLD AGE.

```
G O S S I N O L N H O J
I O C H I L D R E N H A
N B D A B R I E L V A R
C Z E C H A R I A H L C
E D L E L I Z A B E D H
G D I G A L E I G A R A
N B Z U O L E G F H E N
I R A O P S F I A N N G
N I B M O L S X R D S E
R E E G O S S I M B L L
U T T C H I L D P E A O
B G H I N C E N S E B G
```

24

Week 2: Mary – unexpected mother

Thinking about it

What's the point?

God is the true source of life. However much we people – and especially men, even today – may think that we are in charge of things, the real source of everything good is God. And Mary – ordinary, humble Mary – was as surprised as her cousin Elizabeth to find that God had chosen to work a miracle in her life.

Doing it

Prayer

Loving God,
thank you for valuing all of us,
whether we *seem* important or not.
Help us learn to value one another
through the things that we do together.
Amen.

From the known to the unknown

Have the children ever had wonderful surprises – maybe a present, or an outing? God often works in unexpected ways, and sometimes the people he gets to help him in his work would never have expected it.

Tell the story: Luke 1:26-38

(See page 28 for a dramatised version of this story.)

An angel with an angle

Mary was having one of those days – you know, when nothing goes quite the way you expect. She got up that morning, full of good intentions. 'Right,' she thought, making a mental list in her head, 'I've got to mend the goat, milk the cat and take the gate to the vet's – where shall I start? Just a minute, that doesn't sound quite right, to me.'*

'Oh, dear,' she thought, 'that's what happens when your body wakes up before your brain does. Anyway, I'll make a start with that gate – Dad's never going to get round to it. Now, where did I put the hammer?'

'Is this what you're looking for?'

Mary turned to see a very strange-looking man, standing behind the broken gate and leaning on it. She could see he was wearing a pair of blue jeans

* Can the children work out what she meant?

25

(something Mary had never seen before and probably never would again) and a T-shirt with something she couldn't make out written on it, and his hair was short and stood straight up in spikes. Altogether, he seemed a very strange sight to Mary. He smiled at her, mischievously. 'You wanted a hammer, I believe?' He snapped his fingers and a hammer appeared in his hand.

'Neat trick,' said Mary, 'and I suppose you've got some nails handy, too?'

The man looked offended. 'Oh, don't be so mundane,' he said with mock severity. 'Here you are with the Archangel Gabriel right in front of you, and the most exciting thing you can ask for is a box of nails!'

Mary stared. 'Archangel Gabriel? You don't look much like an angel to me.'

'That's what they all say,' said Gabriel, 'but I can't go around in wings and a halo all the time – it's just *so* not cool. I don't want people thinking I'm some sort of poser, now do I?' So saying, he pushed himself off and floated gently up over the gate and back down to the ground, smiling smugly as if to say, 'Look, no wings!'

As he landed he held up a hand modestly. 'No applause, please, this is a solemn moment. Now, I've got to get the next bit right because it'll probably get into the papers or something.' He straightened up, put on a long face that didn't suit him at all, and said, 'Greetings, O favoured one – the Lord is with you.'

Mary stifled a giggle, pulling an exaggeratedly solemn face in the process. 'Don't be afraid, Mary,' Gabriel tried to reassure her. 'God's really pleased with you – like, totally ecstatic, know what I mean? Now, you're going to have a baby – there, how about that, then! He's going to be great – I mean, really mega – and you're to call him Jesus. He'll reign over God's people for – oh, at least – well, for ever, really – probably more with a bit of Providence. And there'll be no end to his kingdom. Good, eh?'

'Terrific,' Mary agreed, 'except that my mum told me it takes two to make a baby, and there's only me.'

'Oh, no prob,' Gabriel said, airily. 'God can do anything he likes – and he's got it all sorted. I mean – oh, do I have to spell it out? – it's going to be God's Son. Look, you know your cousin Elizabeth? The one everyone said couldn't have a baby short of a miracle? Well, she's having one.'

'Baby,' Mary asked, 'or miracle?'

'Well, both, as it goes,' Gabriel answered. 'She's been pregnant for the past six months, now – see what I mean – this is God we're talking about, and the only thing that's impossible for him is nothing.'

Mary was amazed. 'Well!' she exclaimed. 'What can I say?'

'"OK" would be a start,' Gabriel said. 'Or you could be really tedious and demand to see my ID card or something.'

'No need for that,' said Mary. 'I know you're an angel, all right – no one as off-the-wall as you could possibly be mortal.' She took a deep breath. She didn't know what she'd be letting herself in for – or how she was ever going to explain it to her parents – but one thing she did know was that God was doing something pretty cosmic and she had the chance of being right at the heart of it.

'OK, then,' she said. 'You just tell God that I'm up for it. Whatever he wants, he's the boss and I'll do it. Can I go now, please? I've got to go and find Elizabeth so that we can celebrate together. The gate can wait – boy, are we going to party!'

Respond to the story

Discussion

How do the children think Mary felt when she knew she would be the mother of God's Son?

- Flattered?
- Excited?
- Maybe a little nervous?

Song

One or more of the following songs might be used here and/or in the all-age worship:

Be still, for the presence of the Lord
Give thanks with a grateful heart
I'm gonna click, click, click
Make way, make way
Seek ye first the kingdom of God
The angel Gabriel from heaven came

Art and craft

Draw or paint a picture of Mary listening to the angel.

This is the key picture, but you might want to do others in addition to it, such as:

- Mary running to see Elizabeth
- Mary and Elizabeth celebrating together

Drama

See the next page for a dramatised version of the story.

Drama: An angel with an angle

Narrator	Mary was having one of those days – you know, when nothing goes quite the way you expect. She got up that morning, full of good intentions.
Mary	Right, I've got to mend the goat, milk the cat and take the gate to the vet's – where shall I start? Just a minute, that doesn't sound quite right, to me. Oh, dear, that's what happens when your body wakes up before your brain does. Anyway, I'll make a start with that gate – Dad's never going to get round to it. Now, where did I put the hammer?
Gabriel	Is this what you're looking for?
Narrator	Mary turned to see a very strange-looking man, standing behind the broken gate and leaning on it. She could see he was wearing a pair of blue jeans (something Mary had never seen before and probably never would again) and a T-shirt with something she couldn't make out written on it, and his hair was short and stood straight up in spikes. Altogether, he seemed a very strange sight to Mary. He smiled at her, mischievously.
Gabriel	You wanted a hammer, I believe?
Narrator	He snapped his fingers and a hammer appeared in his hand.
Mary	Neat trick, and I suppose you've got some nails handy, too?
Gabriel	[Looking offended] Oh, don't be so mundane! Here you are with the Archangel Gabriel right in front of you, and the most exciting thing you can ask for is a box of nails!
Mary	Archangel Gabriel? You don't look much like an angel to me.
Gabriel	That's what they all say, but I can't go around in wings and a halo all the time – it's just so not cool. I don't want people thinking I'm some sort of poser, now do I?
Narrator	So saying, he pushed himself off and floated gently up, over the gate and back down to the ground, smiling smugly as if to say, 'Look, no wings!' As he landed he held up a hand modestly.
Gabriel	No applause, please, this is a solemn moment. Now, I've got to get the next bit right because it'll probably get into the papers or something.
Narrator	He straightened up, and put on a long face that didn't suit him at all.
Narrator	Greetings, O favoured one – the Lord is with you.
Narrator	Mary stifled a giggle, pulling an exaggeratedly solemn face in the process.
Gabriel	Don't be afraid, Mary, God's really pleased with you – like, totally ecstatic, know what I mean? Now, you're going to have a baby – there, how about that, then! He's going to be great – I mean, really mega – and you're to call him Jesus. He'll reign over God's people for – oh, at least – well, for ever, really – probably more with a bit of Providence. And there'll be no end to his kingdom. Good, eh?

Mary	Terrific, except that my mum told me it takes two to make a baby, and there's only me.
Gabriel	Oh, no prob, God can do anything he likes – and he's got it all sorted. I mean – oh, do I have to spell it out? – it's going to be God's Son. Look, you know your cousin Elizabeth? The one everyone said couldn't have a baby short of a miracle? Well, she's having one.
Mary	Baby, or miracle?
Gabriel	Well, both, as it goes. She's been pregnant for the past six months, now – see what I mean – this is God we're talking about, and the only thing that's impossible for him is nothing.
Mary	[*Amazed*] Well! What can I say?
Gabriel	'OK' would be a start. Or you could be really tedious and demand to see my ID card or something.
Mary	No need for that, I know you're an angel, all right – no one as off-the-wall as you could possibly be mortal.
Narrator	Mary took a deep breath. She didn't know what she'd be letting herself in for – or how she was ever going to explain it to her parents – but one thing she did know was that God was doing something pretty cosmic and she had the chance of being right at the heart of it.
Mary	OK, then, you just tell God that I'm up for it. Whatever he wants, he's the boss and I'll do it. Can I go now, please? I've got to go and find Elizabeth so that we can celebrate together. The gate can wait – boy, are we going to party!

His kingdom will never end!

Help Mary get to Elizabeth, to celebrate.

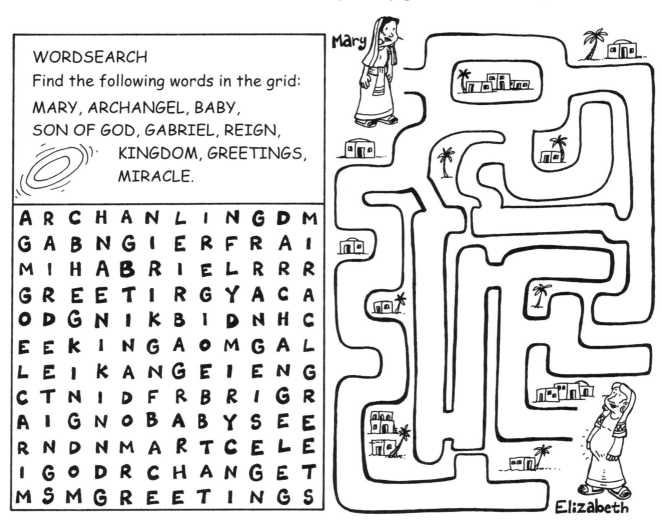

WORDSEARCH

Find the following words in the grid:

MARY, ARCHANGEL, BABY,
SON OF GOD, GABRIEL, REIGN,
KINGDOM, GREETINGS,
MIRACLE.

```
A R C H A N L I N G D M
G A B N G I E R F R A I
M I H A B R I E L R R R
G R E E T I R G Y A C A
O D G N I K B I D N H C
E E K I N G A O M G A L
L E I K A N G E I E N G
C T N I D F R B R I G R
A I G N O B A B Y S E E
R N D N M A R T C E L E
I G O D R C H A N G E T
M S M G R E E T I N G S
```

Week 3: Shepherds – unexpected guests

Thinking about it

What's the point?

Shepherds were left out of everything in Bible days. They were unpopular (they weren't always fussy over whose land they led their sheep in search of pasture) and spent most of their time in a state of being ritually unclean. They were also physically isolated for much of their time, working unsocial hours in remote places. So all ways round they were not the people you'd expect to be at the top of God's guest list – they weren't even *on* anybody else's!

Doing it

Prayer

Loving God,
thank you for showing us
that our ideas about what makes people important
aren't the same as yours.
Thank you for wanting all of us around you,
and please help us to grow in our love for one another.
Amen.

From the known to the unknown

Have the children ever been left out when they felt they ought to have been included – perhaps from an activity at school, or in play with neighbours and friends? God cares about people who feel like that – and here's a story about some people who felt left out all the time – until . . .

Tell the story: Luke 2:8-20

(See page 34 for a dramatised version of this story.)

God's gentle revolution

Abi and Sam were shepherds, and they both wanted a change. 'It's not the job itself,' Sam said, 'I just don't like being looked down on all the time.'

Abi tried to encourage him. 'Don't worry, Sam,' she said. 'Come the revolution *we'll* be calling the shots.'

'Oh, you and your revolution!' scoffed Sam. 'You've got to change people's *attitudes* – and no revolution is going to do that. No, shepherds have always been the bottom of the heap and we always will be. Face it, Abi – no one wants us, not nowhere, not nohow.'

'Now, what sort of a way is that to speak?' came a voice. 'Just because you're a shepherd doesn't mean you have to talk nonsense!' Abi and Sam stared in amazement; the speaker was about ten feet tall, in a long white robe with a pair of enormous wings and a ring of light around his head that lit up the entire night sky.

31

Abi and Sam threw themselves flat on the ground in fear. 'It's God, come to punish us,' Sam trembled. 'It's all your fault, going on about revolutions and things.'

'Well, if you didn't moan all the time . . .,' Abi retorted.

'Oh dear,' said the angel. 'I was afraid this would happen. That's the trouble with ceremonial dress, it frightens people. Look, I can't change in the middle of a mission – it's not allowed – but just don't be frightened, OK? I've got good news for you.'

Slowly, Abi and Sam raised their heads. 'Good news?'

The angel didn't look so terrifying any more – just impressive. 'Sure thing,' he said. 'Good news for you and for the whole world. It's about your Saviour – you know, the one everyone's been on about for centuries? Well, he's here – well, near here – in Bethlehem, to be exact.'

Abi was thrilled. 'That's it – it's started,' she crowed. 'Up the revolution!'

'Oh, you and your revolutions!' scoffed Sam. 'Don't you know a hallucination when you see one?'

The angel interrupted. 'Oh, it's true enough – you don't think I get all dolled up like this for just any old ceremony, do you? I mean, this is really mega – and I suppose it is a *kind* of revolution, but not the kind you're after. *You're* the ones God wants to be the first to know. He's chosen *you* to be the first visitors. I mean, the priests aren't even going to be told, and the king's being kept well in the dark – I'd say that was pretty revolutionary! Go to Bethlehem and look for a baby wrapped in strips of cloth and lying in a donkey's feeding trough. You don't get many of those to the postal district, so you'll know it's the right one.'

The angel raised his hands and snapped his fingers. 'Cue music!' Instantly, the night air was filled with the most wonderful singing – it was a kind of mixture of every different sort of music they'd ever heard – and quite a lot that they hadn't, as well. And for some reason, it all sounded great together! The angel raised his hand again. 'And . . . action!'

'Good grief!' exclaimed Abi. 'There's thousands of them!' And there were – angels stacked up as far as the eye could see, singing, dancing and generally making whoopee. 'Glory to God in heaven!' they thundered. 'Peace to his people on earth!' Peace? No chance, with all that racket! Strangely, though, the sheep didn't seem at all frightened – just went on chewing the grass as though nothing was happening.

'No one else can hear it!' Sam exclaimed – 'All this is being laid on just for us.'

Abi was as amazed as Sam. 'They wouldn't allow that kind of stuff in the synagogue,' she said, as a troupe of angels did a conga across the horizon, while another group rocked to the heavy beat of some instruments Sam and Abi had never seen before. Gradually, the music and the angels became more distant – their last sight was of the angel who'd talked to them high-kicking his way into the nearest cloud. 'Come on!' Sam gasped. 'Let's go to Bethlehem.'

Suddenly, minding the sheep didn't seem so important. They set off on the trot, expecting to find a party in full swing, but when they got there, there were just the parents and the baby. Sam and Abi were awe-struck. 'So all that was just for us!' said Sam. 'So much for not being important!'

Abi looked puzzled. 'I don't know what's going on,' she said, 'but I'm sure it's *some* kind of revolution.'

Respond to the story

Discussion

Can the children remember why Abi wanted a revolution?

- To give her a chance to be important?
- So that she could make people look up to her, instead of down?

Why did Sam think a revolution wouldn't work?

- Because you have to change people's attitudes?
- Because you can't force people to like you?

Song

One or more of the following songs might be used here and/or in the all-age worship:

Come and join the celebration
God was born on earth
Hee, haw! Hee, haw!
See him lying on a bed of straw
There's a star in the East (Rise up, shepherd, and follow)
While shepherds watched

. . . and anything else you care to think of – you hardly need me to suggest songs for Christmas Day, I'm sure!

Art and craft

✔ Prepare the outfits and props for a simple role play. (See 'Word and action' in the All-age worship for how this will be used.) The children could dress up in elaborate costumes or could use simple, representative props or badges; for example: a homeless beggar with a notice slung round the neck saying, 'Two children to support' and a begging bowl in hand; an unemployed person could just carry a placard saying, 'Work wanted – cheap rates'; someone else could carry a notice saying, 'Fresh horse manure, £1 per bag'. (Perhaps the children can think of other examples of people who would be less than welcome in many places.) The 'postie' simply needs a bag, a badge saying 'Royal Mail', and of course a letter to hand to you.

✔ Beyond this, you can be as elaborate as you like, but don't forget to leave time to prepare the children for their role in the service.

Draw or paint a picture of the shepherds around the manger.

This is the key picture, but you might want to do others as well, such as:

- the shepherds shivering on the hillside
- the angel talking to the shepherds
- the choir of angels

Drama: God's gentle revolution

Narrator	Abi and Sam were shepherds, and they both wanted a change.
Sam	It's not the job itself. I just don't like being looked down on all the time.
Abi	Don't worry, Sam – come the revolution *we'll* be calling the shots.
Sam	Oh, you and your revolution! You've got to change people's *attitudes* – and no revolution is going to do that. No, shepherds have always been the bottom of the heap and we always will be. Face it, Abi – no one wants us, not nowhere, not nohow.
Angel	Now, what sort of a way is that to speak? Just because you're a shepherd doesn't mean you have to talk nonsense!
Narrator	Abi and Sam stared in amazement; the speaker was about ten feet tall, in a long white robe with a pair of enormous wings and a ring of light around his head that lit up the entire night sky. Abi and Sam threw themselves flat on the ground in fear.
Sam	God's sent an angel to punish us. It's all your fault, going on about revolutions and things.
Abi	Well, if you didn't moan all the time . . .
Angel	Oh dear, I was afraid this would happen. That's the trouble with ceremonial dress, it frightens people. Look, I can't change in the middle of a mission – it's not allowed – but just don't be frightened, OK? I've got good news for you.
Abi and Sam	Good news?
Narrator	The angel didn't look so terrifying any more – just impressive.
Angel	Sure thing. Good news for you and for the whole world. It's about your Saviour – you know, the one everyone's been on about for centuries? Well, he's here – well, near here – in Bethlehem, to be exact.
Abi	That's it – it's started! Up the revolution!
Sam	Oh, you and your revolutions! Don't you know a hallucination when you see one?
Angel	Oh, it's true enough – you don't think I get all dolled up like this for just any old ceremony, do you? I mean, this is really mega – and I suppose it is a *kind* of revolution, but not the kind you're after. *You're* the ones God wants to be the first to know. He's chosen *you* to be the first visitors. I mean, the priests aren't even going to be told, and the king's being kept well in the dark – I'd say that was pretty revolutionary! Go to Bethlehem and look for a baby wrapped in strips of cloth and lying in a donkey's feeding trough. You don't get many of those to the postal district, so you'll know it's the right one.

Narrator	The angel raised his hands and snapped his fingers.
Angel	Cue music!
Narrator	Instantly, the night air was filled with the most wonderful singing – it was a kind of mixture of every different sort of music they'd ever heard – and quite a lot that they hadn't, as well. And for some reason, it all sounded great together! The angel raised his hand again.
Angel	And . . . action!
Abi	Good grief! There's thousands of them!
Narrator	And there were – angels stacked up as far as the eye could see, singing, dancing and generally making whoopee.
Chorus*	Glory to God in heaven! Peace to his people on earth!
Narrator	Peace? No chance, with all that racket! Strangely, though, the sheep didn't seem at all frightened – just went on chewing the grass as though nothing was happening. Then Sam realised.
Sam	No one else can hear it! It's just for us – all this is being laid on just for us.
Abi	[*Amazed*] They wouldn't allow that kind of stuff in the synagogue.
Narrator	As she spoke, a troupe of angels was doing a conga across the horizon while another group rocked to the heavy beat of some instruments Sam and Abi had never seen before. Gradually, the music and the angels became more distant – their last sight was of the angel who'd talked to them high-kicking his way into the nearest cloud.
Sam	Come on! Let's go to Bethlehem.
Narrator	Suddenly, minding the sheep didn't seem so important. They set off on the trot, expecting to find a party in full swing, but when they got there, there were just the parents and the baby. Sam and Abi were awe-struck.
Sam	So all that was just for us! So much for not being important!
Abi	I don't know what's going on, but I'm sure it's *some* kind of revolution.

* A chance, if a brief one, for everybody to be involved!

Glory to God in the highest! (Luke 2:14)

These pictures look the same,
but can you find 6 differences?

WORDSEARCH

Find the following words in the grid:

GLORY TO GOD, PEACE ON EARTH, SHEPHERDS, CHOSEN, WATCH, ANGELS, SHEEP, SINGING, FEEDING TROUGH, BETHLEHEM.

```
G L O R Y T O G O D S P
N W F E E D I N G T H E
I E A S I N G I N R E A
G E N T G U O R T O P C
N D G E C N G I O U H E
I I E S N H E L R G E O
S N R C H S O S Y H R N
B G T H L E H E O M T E
S D R E H P E H S H S A
A N G B E T H P E H C R
A N G E T N I G N I S T
A R M E H E L H T E B H
```

Week 4: Christmas all-age worship

Opening song

Welcome and statement of the theme

Get one or more of the children to point out or hold up the pictures as you sum up the story:

In Junior Church during the past few weeks, we've been getting ready for Christmas by looking at how God surprised everyone by the way he worked. Zechariah and Elizabeth had never been able to have any children, and everybody thought they were now too old. But they became the parents of John the Baptist who was sent to announce Jesus' coming. Then God chose Mary, a very ordinary young woman, who didn't even have a husband – and you really needed one of those if you wanted to have a baby. But God worked a miracle for her and gave her a central part to play in his greatest-ever story. Finally, we came to the Christmas story itself, and we saw the surprising people God chose to celebrate with – not the people we might have expected, like priests and governors, and not just 'ordinary' people, either – he chose some people who were really looked down on in polite society – shepherds. So this Christmas we're celebrating God's presence in the world in unexpected things.

Prayer

Loving God,
we praise you for coming into the world
and into our lives –
for caring about us enough
to share with us in all our experiences.
We thank you for Jesus,
who came to show us your love
in ways that still challenge us
as well as fill us with joy.
Please forgive us for the times we forget how great your love is,
and when we treat some people as less important.
Help us to remember that everyone is important to you –
and especially help us to remember, and to celebrate,
that that means us.
Thank you, Loving God,
for all that this season means to us.
Amen.

Word and action

Have the actors waiting out of sight, and start by telling the congregation that you're very excited because you're expecting a personal visit from Jesus himself. The first actor knocks, and you excitedly call, 'Come in', only to look disappointed when one of the actors enters. Immediately hustle him or her out again, saying something like, 'We don't want Jesus getting the wrong impression, do we?'

Repeat this, with slight variations, until all the characters except the postie have been in. When the postie knocks and enters, you can look surprised – who would be sending you a letter on Christmas Day? Open the letter and read out:

Dear (Your name)

I'm so sorry to have embarrassed you by inviting my friends along – I thought you would be pleased, but obviously I misunderstood. So as to avoid causing you any more distress, I'll just go somewhere else – I really don't want to be any trouble.

All my love to you all,

Jesus.

PS Happy Christmas!

Now you can act suitably chastened, and ask the actors to return before pointing out that all the time you were excitedly waiting for Jesus, he was already here – but not in quite the form you were expecting!

Now, have the story from Week 3 read, in either narrative or dramatised form.

Song 2

Offering

This may be introduced as symbolising our response to the incredible love God shows us in coming to share our lives.

Offertory prayer

Holy God,
as you offer yourself to us in simple ways,
so we bring our simple offering to you.
Help us so to offer ourselves and our gifts
that the world around us may recognise you
at the very heart of its life.
Amen.

Song 3

Reading

Isaiah 42:1-9 read from a standard Bible. Introduce it with words such as: Through the prophet Isaiah, God promises a Saviour whose rule will be based on gentleness and love, and yet who will radically transform the world.

Talk (optional)

If you feel it appropriate (and if time permits) you might point out that both the prophecy and the event were two-edged: gentle and comforting, yet radical and challenging. God does not merely comfort the oppressed, but exalts them – and that's going to be a threat to somebody else! So the gospel is not of a 'love' that's just nice to people, but a love that also challenges our assumptions and threatens to make a difference!

Notices and family news

Prayers of intercession

These could be led entirely by the minister or other adult(s), and/or could include some prayers written by the children themselves – or simply some points that they have raised in discussion.

Song 4

Closing prayer/benediction

Unit 2
Journeying to Easter

Overview of the unit

Theme: Through death to new life

We take three key events:

Week 1: Crossing the Red Sea

We hear the story of the Israelites' journey from the old life of slavery to the new life of freedom and hope.

Week 2: The Garden of Gethsemane

Jesus agonises over the journey now ahead of him. Will he go in faith, or will he pull back at the last moment?

Week 3: Journey's end – new life!

The journey ends at Easter: the people who have 'followed' Jesus all the way are the first to discover the Good News.

Easter Sunday all-age worship

This will focus on the Easter story – not the Red Sea or the Garden of Gethsemane – so the theme of the service will come from Week 3, emphasised in the 'Word and action' material. Some of the art and craft work the children have done in the other weeks will be used to decorate the church and set the wider context of the story, emphasising the idea of *going through* rather than coming back, and the challenge of faith that that holds before us.

Week 1: Crossing the Red Sea

Thinking about it

What's the point?

This is a traditional Easter story, and emphasises the concept of Jesus going through death and out the other side to new life (as distinct, incidentally, from Lazarus or Jairus' daughter, for example, who came back to the old life and presumably died again at some stage). So the imagery is of a journey of faith through a dark and threatening stage to a completely new life. If any of the children are currently dealing with bereavement, this could offer the opportunity for some helpful (but discreetly low-key) pastoral work.

Doing it

Prayer

Loving God,
thank you for bringing us together this morning.
Help us to enjoy the time we share
and to learn more of your love.
Amen.

From the known to the unknown

Ask the children to imagine that they're on their way to a party, but they find themselves with an unpleasant dark alley to go through. (Of course, we know the younger ones at any rate would hardly be likely to be out unaccompanied, but this is pretend . . .) Would they go through it alone? Would they ask a passing stranger to help them? Or would they only go through it if they had someone with them whom they knew and trusted?

Tell the story: Exodus 14:10-31

(See page 46 for a dramatised version of this story.)

By faith to new life

The Israelites were giving Moses a hard time. The ringleader was Jes – a real troublemaker. 'We're trapped!' he yelled. 'Egyptians on one side and water on the other – where do we go now?'

'God promised to lead you to freedom,' Moses insisted, 'and he will. Trust me – or rather, trust God.'

'Oh, great!' chipped in Debs. 'So we'll be free, will we? We'll be dead, that's what. We might have been slaves in Egypt but at least we were alive.'

'God will get us through,' Moses promised. 'No one ever said freedom would be easy.'

'Oh, get real!' scoffed Ben. 'The Egyptians are chasing us, and the only way out is blocked by the sea. 'What are you going to do – build a big boat or something? And don't tell us to trust God – he got us into this in the first place.'

Moses had to admit it looked scary. Then he heard God speaking.

'Tell them to stop yelling at me and start moving,' he said. 'Hold out your stick over the sea and I'll make you a dry path to walk on.'

'Come on, you lot,' Moses shouted to all the people. 'Show a bit of faith – start moving, and trust God for the rest.'

The people were still grumbling, but they didn't see any other way, so they started moving forward towards the sea shore. Moses went ahead and held out his stick over the water. The sound of the Egyptians' horses got closer – their hooves drumming on the ground, the chariot wheels rumbling on the sand and clattering over rocks. It was a horrible noise, but gradually a different sound took over – a strong east wind had sprung up, and the once calm waters of the Red Sea were being whipped up into a foaming lather.

'He must be mad,' said Jes. 'If Moses thinks we're going to cross that sea, he must be completely crackers.'

'Oh, don't worry, we won't drown,' said Debs. 'No, the great sea monster will eat us up before we get the chance to drown!'

'Thanks a bunch!' said Jes. 'That makes me feel a whole lot better.'

'Anyway,' Ben added, 'by the time the sea monster gets us, we'll be feeling so awful it'll be a relief to die.'

'Why don't you go and cheer someone else up?' Jes suggested, sarcastically. 'I wouldn't want to be selfish and keep you all to myself.'

By this time, they could hardly hear each other, anyway. The wind was howling, the waves crashing on to the shore, and they were beginning to think that being slaves in Egypt had really been rather wonderful compared with this. And still Moses stood there, like a bizarre statue, with his stick held out over the sea.

'God will help us,' he kept telling himself. 'I'm sure God will help us – won't he?'

'You just stand there,' God answered. 'Leave the work to me. I'm not finished yet by a long way.'

Although it was only a few hours, it seemed like weeks as they stood there, hearing the wind howling and the waves roaring. Then, to everybody's amazement, the sea began to move apart. Only a little at first, but gradually a wide path appeared through the middle of the foaming sea.

'Come on!' shouted Moses, and began to move forwards toward the path God had made. But it was still scary.

'If that wind drops,' shouted Jes, 'we're all dead.'

'And I bet the sea monster's hiding in there,' yelled Debs, 'just waiting to gobble us all up.'

'Well, we've got to face either that or the Egyptians,' Ben shouted in reply.

Gradually, the people moved forward towards the roaring waves and began to walk the path that God had made. For hours, they travelled – all the time fearing that the wind might drop and the waters swallow them up, or that the monster might get them. Then, above the noise of the storm, Ben and his friends heard a shout of joy. The first people had reached the other side. Suddenly, they felt stronger and began to march more briskly, and through the spray they glimpsed the opposite shore where a great celebration was already underway. Someone started singing, and their spirits rose. Soon, they were there – safely across and without even a wet foot between them! What a party they had! People were singing and dancing like mad, and for once Jes wasn't complaining. 'This is *so* the life!' he said. 'No, really – this is *living*!'

Respond to the story

Discussion

How do the children think it would have felt to walk though the water?

- Scary?
- Exciting?

Why do the children think they actually went through?

- Because they trusted Moses?
- Because they trusted God?
- Because staying where they were was also scary?
- A bit of all three?

Song

One or more of the following songs might be used here and/or in the all-age worship:

How did Moses cross the Red Sea
How great is our God
Moses, I know you're the man
One more step along the world I go
We are marching in the light of God

Art and craft

Draw or paint a picture of the people crossing the Red Sea.

This is the key picture, but you might want to do others in addition to it, such as:

- Moses stretching out his stick over the water
- the party on the far side of the sea

Drama

See the next page for a dramatised version of the story.

Drama: By faith to new life

Narrator	The Israelites were giving Moses a hard time. The ringleader was Jes – a real troublemaker.
Jes	We're trapped! Egyptians on one side and water on the other – where do we go now?
Moses	God promised to lead you to freedom, and he will. Trust me – or rather, trust God.
Debs	Oh, great! So we'll be free, will we? We'll be dead, that's what. We might have been slaves in Egypt but at least we were alive.
Moses	God will get us through. No one ever said freedom would be easy.
Ben	Oh, get real! The Egyptians are chasing us, and the only way out is blocked by the sea. What are you going to do – build a big boat or something? And don't tell us to trust God – he got us into this in the first place.
Narrator	Moses had to admit it looked scary. Then he heard God speaking.
God	Tell them to stop yelling at me and start moving. Hold out your stick over the sea and I'll make you a dry path to walk on.
Moses	Come on, you lot, show a bit of faith – start moving, and trust God for the rest.
Narrator	The people were still grumbling, but they didn't see any other way, so they started moving forward towards the sea shore. Moses went ahead and held out his stick over the water. The sound of the Egyptians' horses got closer – their hooves drumming on the ground, the chariot wheels rumbling on the sand and clattering over rocks. It was a horrible noise, but gradually a different sound took over – a strong east wind had sprung up, and the once calm waters of the Red Sea were being whipped up into a foaming lather.
Jes	He must be mad. If Moses thinks we're going to cross that sea, he must be completely crackers.
Debs	Oh, don't worry, we won't drown. No, the great sea monster will eat us up before we get the chance to drown!
Jes	Thanks a bunch! That makes me feel a whole lot better.
Ben	Anyway, by the time the sea monster gets us, we'll be feeling so awful it'll be a relief to die.
Jes	[*Sarcastically*] Why don't you go and cheer someone else up? I wouldn't want to be selfish and keep you all to myself.
Narrator	By this time, they could hardly hear each other, anyway. The wind was howling, the waves crashing on to the shore, and they were beginning to think that being slaves in Egypt had really been rather wonderful compared with this. And still Moses stood there, like a bizarre statue, with his stick held out over the sea.
Moses	God will help us. I'm sure God will help us – won't he?

God   You just stand there. Leave the work to me. I'm not finished yet by a long way.

Narrator   It seemed like weeks as they stood there, hearing the wind howling and the waves roaring. Then, to everybody's amazement, the sea began to move apart. Only a little at first, but gradually a wide path appeared through the middle of the foaming sea.

Moses   [*Shouts*] Come on! Let's go!

Jes   If that wind drops, we're all dead.

Debs   And I bet the sea monster's hiding in there, just waiting to gobble us all up.

Ben   Well, we've got to face either that or the Egyptians.

Narrator   Gradually, the people moved forward towards the roaring waves and began to walk the path that God had made. For hours, they travelled – all the time fearing that the wind might drop and the waters swallow them up, or that the monster might get them. Then, above the noise of the storm, Ben and his friends heard a shout of joy. The first people had reached the other side. Suddenly, they felt stronger and began to march more briskly, and through the spray they glimpsed the opposite shore where a great celebration was already underway. Someone started singing, and their spirits rose. Soon, they were there – safely across and without even a wet foot between them! What a party they had! People were singing and dancing like mad, and for once Jes wasn't complaining.

Jes   This is *so* the life! No, really – this is *living*!

Why do you cry out to me? . . . go forward! (Exodus 14:15)

Crack the code!

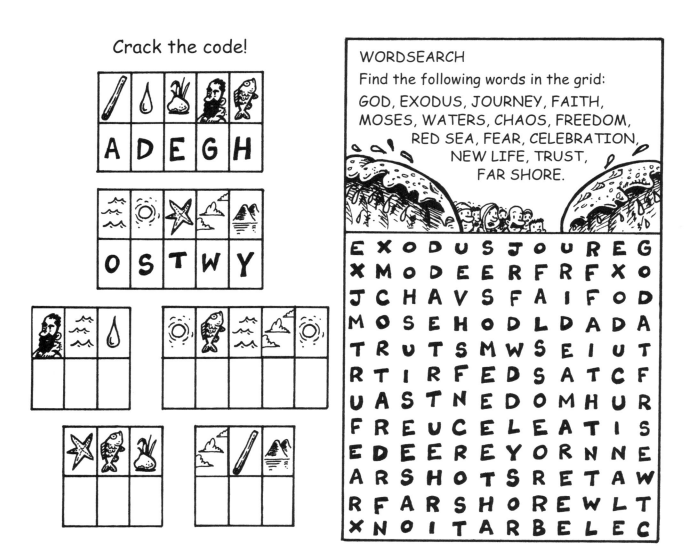				
A	D	E	G	H

O	S	T	W	Y

WORDSEARCH

Find the following words in the grid:

GOD, EXODUS, JOURNEY, FAITH, MOSES, WATERS, CHAOS, FREEDOM, RED SEA, FEAR, CELEBRATION, NEW LIFE, TRUST, FAR SHORE.

```
E X O D U S J O U R E G
X M O D E E R F R F X O
J C H A V S F A I F O D
M O S E H O D L D A D A
T R U T S M W S E I U T
R T I R F E D S A T C F
U A S T N E D O M H U R
F R E U C E L E A T I S
E D E E R E Y O R N N E
A R S H O T S R E T A W
R F A R S H O R E W L T
X N O I T A R B E L E C
```

Week 2: The Garden of Gethsemane

What's the point?

Like the Israelites in last week's story, Jesus has a 'go through or turn back' choice to make. Will he go in faith where his Father is calling him to go, or will he shrink from it? His faith tells him that God will bring him through, but his human instinct is to pull back

Doing it

Prayer

Holy God,
thank you for loving us and always being with us.
Help us to understand that a little better
through the things we do together today,
through Jesus Christ our Lord.
Amen.

From the known to the unknown

Have the children ever experienced doing something that they know is really worthwhile but being tempted to give up because it gets hard? We all face those kinds of moments, and it can be really difficult. The Bible tells us that Jesus knows just how that feels – and then some!

Tell the story: Matthew 26:36-46

(See page 52 for a dramatised version of this story.)

Jesus on the edge

Jesus was very unhappy. Actually, before I go any further, I ought to tell you that this story worked out wonderfully well in the end – like the one we had last week, but even better – but we're not going to get to the happy ending until next week.

Now, where was I? Oh, yes – Jesus was unhappy. He'd just had his last supper with his disciples, and he knew that he was soon going to die. People who hated him were plotting to get rid of him. He trusted his Father God to work things out, but he knew it was going to be very scary and very painful along the way.

'Let's go out,' he said to his disciples, and they all got up from the table to follow him to the Garden of Gethsemane.

'Jesus seems very thoughtful tonight,' Thomas commented as they went. 'I get the feeling something really dreadful's going to happen.'

'Oh, I wouldn't worry,' James assured him. 'God'll keep us safe – he's good like that – he won't let any harm come to Jesus.'

'Well, I don't know,' Thomas replied. 'I trust God, of course, but I don't think it's quite as simple as that.'

By now, they'd arrived in the garden. They'd never seen Jesus look so upset. 'If I didn't know better, I'd say he was frightened,' said Peter.

Jesus spoke. 'Peter, James and John, you come with me. The rest of you, sit here while I go and pray.'

A little further on, he turned to his three friends and said, 'This is a very difficult time for me. Will you watch with me?' Then he went a little further on his own and lay down on the ground to pray. 'Father, this is awful – isn't there some way I can avoid what's going to happen? Isn't there another way?' Then he took a deep breath, and said, 'But it's your will that matters, so I'll go through it if I have to.'

He got up and walked back to his three friends, who had fallen fast asleep. 'Oh, Peter,' he said, 'Couldn't you manage to stay awake for just one hour, to pray with me? Come on, stay awake – pray that you don't have to go through what I'm going to. I know you mean well, but you're just not strong enough to hack it.'

As he went away, the disciples looked at one another. 'What was that all about?' James asked.

'I dunno,' John replied, 'but I wish we could just go home – it's scary here.'

He was right. It was very dark, with the moonlight casting sinister shadows among the trees – but that was nothing compared with the fear that Jesus was feeling as he lay down again to pray to his Father. 'It's not that I don't trust you,' he said, 'but this is such a terrible thing I'm going to have to bear, and I really wish there was another way. Surely, we can avoid it somehow? Still, it's your will that matters, not mine.'

When Jesus went back to his friends, they were completely out of it – fast asleep and dead to the world. This time, he didn't wake them but went and prayed again – saying just the same as before. The silence was terrible. Although he prayed harder than ever he had prayed in his life, there seemed to be no answer. Just that awesome silence – not even the rustling of the usual wildlife or the movement of the breeze. Nothing. It was as if all creation was holding its breath to see what Jesus would do.

Jesus knew what he had to do. But knowing didn't make it easy. For what seemed like hours he lay there on the ground, praying, but all his words seemed just to vanish into the still, horrible silence of the night. Eventually, he got up and went back to his sleeping friends. 'Time to wake up,' he said. 'This is it – I've got to do what God sent me to do. Look, they've come to get me.'

Suddenly, the garden was full of people with swords and sticks, all looking for Jesus. Jesus faced up to them calmly. 'I'm the one you want,' he said. 'Let my friends go.' Peter wanted to make a fight of it, and pulled out a sword; but Jesus stopped him. 'I've preached love and non-violence all my ministry,' he said, 'and I'm not going to throw all that away just to save my own skin.'

So Jesus was captured and led away, and his friends turned and ran.

Jesus had made his choice. He stayed true to God, and true to his own faith. Even as they nailed him to the cross, he prayed for them and kept on trusting God. When he died, some people thought it was all over – but it wasn't. He'd won the battle – he'd kept faith with God even when everything seemed hopeless. And now, God was going to keep faith with him – soon he would be raised to wonderful new life. And that's the story for next week. Don't miss it!

Respond to the story

Discussion

Why do the children think Jesus asked his friends to watch and pray with him?

- Because he needed encouragement?
- Because he valued their prayers?
- Because it was too dreadful a time to be on his own?

How might he have felt when he found they had fallen asleep?

- Sad?
- Disappointed?
- Would he have understood how hard it was for them, as well?

Song

One or more of the following songs might be used here and/or in the all-age worship:

Lord, the light of your love is shining
O Lord, hear my prayer
One more step along the world I go
Peace, perfect peace is the gift of Christ our Lord
Shalom, my friends
When I needed a neighbour were you there?

Art and craft

Draw or paint a picture of Jesus praying in the garden.

This is the key picture, but you might want to do others in addition to it, such as:

- people coming to arrest Jesus
- the cross on the hilltop

Drama

See the next page for a dramatised version of the story.

Drama: Jesus on the edge

(Before you begin, make sure the point made at the start of the narrative version is driven home. This story is sad and rather threatening – children need to know there's a happy ending, even though they won't actually get to it this week.)

Narrator Jesus was very unhappy. He'd just had his last supper with his disciples, and he knew that he was soon going to die. People who hated him were plotting to get rid of him. He trusted his Father God to work things out, but he knew it was going to be very scary and very painful along the way. His disciples followed as he got up from the table and led them to the Garden of Gethsemane. Thomas was worried.

Thomas Jesus seems very thoughtful tonight, James. I get the feeling something really dreadful's going to happen.

James Oh, I wouldn't worry, Thomas. God'll keep us safe – he's good like that – he won't let any harm come to Jesus.

Thomas Well, I don't know. I trust God of course, but I don't think it's quite as simple as that.

Narrator By now, they'd arrived in the garden. They'd never seen Jesus look so upset – and it was Peter's turn to be worried.

Peter If I didn't know better, I'd say he was frightened.

Jesus Peter, James and John, you come with me. The rest of you, sit here while I go and pray.

Narrator Jesus led his three closest friends a little further on.

Jesus This is a very difficult time for me. Will you watch with me?

Narrator Then Jesus went a little further on his own and lay down on the ground to pray.

Jesus Father, this is awful – isn't there some way I can avoid what's going to happen? Isn't there another way? But it's your will that matters, so I'll go through it if I have to.

Narrator He got up and walked back to his three friends, who had fallen fast asleep.

Jesus Oh, Peter, couldn't you manage to stay awake for just one hour, to pray with me? Come on, stay awake – pray that you don't have to go through what I'm going to. I know you mean well, but you're just not strong enough to hack it.

Narrator As he went way, the disciples looked at one another in bewilderment.

James What was that all about?

John I dunno, but I wish we could just go home – it's scary here.

Narrator He was right. It was very dark, with the moonlight casting sinister shadows among the trees – but that was nothing compared with the fear that Jesus was feeling as he lay down again to pray to his Father.

Jesus	It's not that I don't trust you, Father, but this is such a terrible thing I'm going to have to bear, and I really wish there was another way. Surely, we can avoid it somehow? Still, it's your will that matters, not mine.
Narrator	When Jesus went back to his friends, they were completely out of it – fast asleep and dead to the world. This time, he didn't wake them but went and prayed again – saying just the same as before. The silence was terrible. Although he prayed harder than ever he had prayed in his life, there seemed to be no answer. Just that awesome silence – not even the rustling of the usual wildlife or the movement of the breeze. Nothing. It was as if all creation was holding its breath to see what Jesus would do. Jesus knew what he had to do. But knowing didn't make it easy. For what seemed like hours he lay there on the ground, praying, but all his words seemed just to vanish into the still, horrible silence of the night. Eventually, he got up and went back to his sleeping friends.
Jesus	Time to wake up. This is it – I've got to do what God sent me to do. Look, they've come to get me.
Narrator	Suddenly, the garden was full of people with swords and sticks, all looking for Jesus. Jesus faced up to them calmly.
Jesus	I'm the one you want. Let my friends go.
Narrator	Peter wanted to make a fight of it, and pulled out a sword; but Jesus stopped him.
Jesus	I've preached love and non-violence all my ministry, and I'm not going to throw all that away just to save my own skin.
Narrator	So Jesus was captured and led away, and his friends turned and ran. Jesus had made his choice. He stayed true to God, and true to his own faith. Even as they nailed him to the cross, he prayed for them and kept on trusting God. When he died, some people thought it was all over – but it wasn't. He'd won the battle – he'd kept faith with God even when everything seemed hopeless. And now, God was going to keep faith with him – soon he would be raised to wonderful new life. And that's the story for next week. Let's not miss it!

Jesus' friends are hiding because they're afraid. Can you spot them in the picture?

I am with you always. (Matthew 28:20)

WORDSEARCH
Find the following words in the grid:

GETHSEMANE, JESUS, DARKNESS, WATCH, WAIT, PRAY, SILENCE, FAITH, OBEDIENT, GARDEN, FEAR, TRUST, HOPE, NEW LIFE.

Week 3: Journey's end – new life!

Thinking about it

What's the point?

The first people to learn about resurrection are the women who stuck with Jesus all the way through. Often we feel like running away when life gets difficult – but if we run away from the pain, we're probably running away from the hope, too – because that's where it's going to be born!

Doing it

Prayer

Loving God,
we've come together to learn about your promise
of new life and new hope.
Help us to enjoy what we do,
and to find your love in the friendships we share.
Amen.

From the known to the unknown

Ask the children to imagine having a friend (or sibling) who's in some kind of difficulty – perhaps they're having a hard time at school, or perhaps they're very ill. Being with them isn't as much fun as it used to be – in fact, it might be very unpleasant. Would they stand by them? When Jesus was in trouble, the friends who stood by him were the first ones to know when the Good News came.

Tell the story: Luke 23:44-24:11

(See page 58 for a dramatised version of this story.)

He's alive!

Jesus' enemies thought they'd won when they saw him nailed to the cross, but they couldn't have been more wrong. Even there, Jesus showed that love can be stronger than hatred. He never cursed anyone – he even prayed for the people who were torturing him – and he comforted the criminal who was dying on the cross next to him. And the last words he said were words of faith. 'Father,' he said, 'I commend my soul into your care.'

Standing at the foot of the cross was a tough soldier – a hard man, who'd seen a lot of death – and even he couldn't help being impressed. 'What a man!' he said. 'He truly was a completely good man!'

Standing further away were some of the women who were friends of Jesus. They'd never left him, even at the most dangerous moments, but had stayed there to show they cared. 'You ought to go home,' said a passing man. 'This is no place for women.'

Joanna, one of the women, answered, 'Well, someone has to be here to share his last moments with him – we're not going to let him die alone.' Then, when they knew Jesus was dead, she turned to Mary Magdalene and said, 'Let's go and see where they bury him – then we can come back later to pay our respects.'

Stealthily, not wanting to attract attention, they followed the men who were burying Jesus. They saw him placed hurriedly in a hole in the hillside, with a big stone rolled in front to seal it. 'After the religious festival's over,' said Mary, 'we'll come back and make sure he's given a *decent* burial.'

So it was that, early on the Sunday morning, the same women – Joanna, Mary Magdalene and the other Mary who was James' mother – all met with jars of spice and perfume to go to Jesus' grave. 'How are we going to move that big stone away from the grave?' asked Mary Magdalene.

'I don't know,' said the other Mary. 'Let's worry about that when we get there.'

'A lot of people would say we were mad, anyway,' Joanna commented, 'but these things matter. Jesus always cared about other people, so now we're going to do the right thing by him.'

They walked silently in the early dawn light until they came within sight of the tomb, and they stopped in amazement and horror. 'Someone's opened it already,' gasped Joanna. 'The stone's been rolled away.'

'Someone's up to no good,' Mary Magdalene murmured quietly. 'Can't they just let him rest in peace?'

Slowly, they moved nearer to the tomb and peered in. It looked very spooky, but as their eyes became used to the low light they saw something that made them stop in their tracks.

Nothing.

Jesus' body wasn't there.

They were staring open-mouthed at one another when suddenly the place was filled with light, and two men in dazzling white clothes stood in front of them. 'Why are you looking in a grave for someone who's alive?' one of them asked. 'Jesus isn't here – he's risen from the dead!' The women were terrified, but gradually the truth sank in as the man continued talking. 'Remember what he told you while he was with you before – how he'd be killed by his enemies but would rise again on the third day? Well, this is it!'

Suddenly, everything fell into place. Of course – God had raised Jesus to new life, just as Jesus had said that he would. The women didn't know whether to laugh or cry for joy!

'Fancy us being the first to know,' exclaimed Mary Magdalene.

'Not so surprising,' Joanna replied. 'After all, we stayed with him – and we're here now.'

'Come on!' cried the other Mary. 'We've got to tell the others.'

What a sight they were – stumbling over tree roots, tripping over the hems of their skirts, and laughing joyfully all the time, as they ran to where they knew the disciples were hiding. 'He's alive! he's alive! Really, he is – just as he promised he would be!'

At first, none of the men believed them – they thought the women had been dreaming or something. But they hadn't – and soon the whole world was going to be buzzing with the Good News: Jesus is alive!

Respond to the story

Discussion

How do the children think the women felt when they found Jesus was alive?

- Joyful?
- Awestruck?
- A bit nervous, perhaps?

How do the children think the women felt when the men didn't believe them?

- Angry?
- Frustrated?
- Confident that they would be proved right in the end?

Song

One or more of the following songs might be used here and/or in the all-age worship:

Alleluia, alleluia, give thanks to the risen Lord
I danced in the morning
Sing a song, sing a joyful song
The women went to Jesus' tomb
This is the day, this is the day

Art and craft

✔ Prepare for an Easter procession. (See 'Word and action' in the All-age worship for how this would be used.) You will need a processional cross – if the church has one you might be able to use that, or if not make a simple one from two lengths of wood. Don't make it too big or heavy – for this service it needs to be clear that it isn't a burden but a symbol of liberation. Plan where the procession will go, and designate a child to lead it (but point out that they're all going to be leaders – they're going to lead the congregation on a journey to new life!) If the route takes you through a few doors that's all the better. This can be done very simply, or it could be made more powerfully symbolic if your building and resources are appropriate. For example, would your circumstances lend themselves to the idea of having some black curtains hung over the door leading out of the church? Another refinement would be to have a screen, using either a sheet of tissue-paper or just a few strips that could be taped across the doorway by which you will return – then you would be able to go through the dark curtains of 'death' and burst through the barrier on the way back, symbolising the breakthrough to new life! However simple or complicated you make it, keep the central point in mind: the journey to new life.

Draw or paint a picture of the women at the empty tomb.

This is the key picture, but you might want to do others in addition to it, such as:

- the women preparing to set out in the early dawn
- the women running to tell the others about Jesus' resurrection

Drama: He's alive!

Narrator	Jesus' enemies thought they'd won when they saw him nailed to the cross, but they couldn't have been more wrong. Even there, Jesus showed that love can be stronger than hatred. He never cursed anyone – he even prayed for the people who were torturing him – and he comforted the criminal who was dying on the cross next to him. And the last words he said were words of faith.
Jesus	Father, I commend my soul into your care.
Narrator	Standing at the foot of the cross was a tough soldier – a hard man, who'd seen a lot of death – and even he couldn't help being impressed.
Soldier	What a man! He truly was a completely good man!
Narrator	Standing further away were some of the women who were friends of Jesus. They'd never left him, even at the most dangerous moments, but had stayed there to show they cared.
Passer-by (male)	You ought to go home. This is no place for women.
Joanna	Well, someone has to be here to share his last moments with him – we're not going to let him die alone.
Narrator	Joanna was there with Mary Magdalene and another Mary, the mother of James, who all felt the same way. When they finally knew Jesus was dead, she turned to Mary Magdalene.
Joanna	Let's go and see where they bury him.
Magdalene	Yes – then we can come back later to pay our respects.
Narrator	Stealthily, not wanting to attract attention, they followed the men who were burying Jesus. They saw him placed hurriedly in a hole in the hillside, with a big stone rolled in front to seal it.
Mary	After the religious festival's over, we'll come back and make sure he's given a *decent* burial.
Narrator	So it was that, early on the Sunday morning, the same women – Joanna, Mary Magdalene and the other Mary who was James' mother – all met with jars of spice and perfume to go to Jesus' grave.
Magdalene	How are we going to move that big stone away from the grave?
Mary	I don't know – let's worry about that when we get there.
Joanna	A lot of people would say we were mad, anyway, but these things matter. Jesus always cared about other people, so now we're going to do the right thing by him.
Narrator	They walked silently in the early dawn light until they came within sight of the tomb, and they stopped in amazement and horror.

Joanna	Someone's opened it already. The stone's been rolled away.
Magdalene	Someone's up to no good. Can't they just let him rest in peace?
Narrator	Slowly, they moved nearer to the tomb and peered in. It looked very spooky, but as their eyes became used to the low light they saw something that made them stop in their tracks. Nothing. Jesus' body wasn't there. They were staring open-mouthed at one another when suddenly the place was filled with light, and two men in dazzling white clothes stood in front of them.
First man	Why are you looking in a grave for someone who's alive?
Second man	Jesus isn't here – he's risen from the dead!
Narrator	The women were terrified, but gradually the truth sank in as the men continued talking.
First man	Remember what he told you while he was with you before – how he'd be killed by his enemies but would rise again on the third day?
Second man	Well, this is it!
Narrator	Suddenly, everything fell into place. Of course – God had raised Jesus to new life, just as Jesus had said that he would. The women didn't know whether to laugh or cry for joy!
Magdalene	Fancy us being the first to know!
Joanna	Not so surprising. After all, we stayed with him – and we're here now.
Mary	Come on! We've got to tell the others.
Narrator	What a sight they were – stumbling over tree roots, tripping over the hems of their skirts, and laughing joyfully all the time, as they ran to where they knew the disciples were hiding.
Mary	He's alive! he's alive! Really, he is – just as he promised he would be!
Narrator	At first, none of the men believed them – they thought they'd been dreaming or something. But they hadn't – and soon the whole world was going to be buzzing with the Good News: Jesus is alive!

Colour the dotted shapes.

Help the women get to the tomb.

WORDSEARCH
Find the following words in the grid:
MAGDALENE, JOANNA, MOTHER,
WOMEN, CROSS, SUNDAY, JESUS,
RESURRECTION, TOMB, STONE,
GOOD NEWS, SPICES, SOLDIER.

```
M A G D A L E N E O T S
O M B W O L D I E R T J
T V G O O D N E W S O E
H J D G A M O T H A M S
E E E S U R E T N E B S
R S P S I C F N O R M S
X U J E U S A C D E O E
C T N E V S O R A I S C
S U N D A Y G O L D P I
G O O E N O T S E L I P
R E S U R R E S N O R S
N O I T C E R R U S E R
```

Week 4: Easter Sunday all-age worship

Opening song

A song praising and celebrating the faithfulness of God

Welcome and statement of the theme

Get one or more of the children to point out or hold up the pictures as you sum up the story:

In Junior Church during the past few weeks, we've been learning about how God can lead us through fear to hope and to new life. We looked at the Red Sea story, and saw how the Israelites were called to make a journey into the unknown, trusting in God to bring them safely through to the other side – a story that foreshadows the much greater journey Jesus made through death to new life on the other side, trusting in his heavenly Father. Then we turned to Jesus, and saw him in the garden of Gethsemane preparing to make that journey – and how hard it was, even for him. And, of course, we finished up at Easter where we saw that those who had, in some sort of way, shared his journey by staying faithful to him were the first to discover the good news of Jesus' resurrection.

That's the general picture, but today, of course, we're going to concentrate on the Easter story itself.

Prayer

Loving God,
giver of all life and hope,
we praise and thank you this morning
for the wonderful news of Jesus' resurrection,
and for the promise that we too can have new life in him.
We thank you for giving us foretastes of that new life,
here on earth,
and for the promise that we shall share it
in all its wonder and glory in eternity.
Forgive us for the times when we don't trust you enough,
and we shrink back from difficult steps
that you are calling us to take,
and help us to trust in you for hope and renewal,
through Jesus Christ our risen and living Lord.
Amen.

Word and action

Have the story from Week 3 read, either in narrative or dramatised form.

Explain to the congregation that you are going to invite them to follow the children in acting out the journey to new life. Everyone is invited to join in, but if (as will almost inevitably be the case) there are those who would find it difficult, they are free simply to stay seated and use the time to pray for people who, in real life, are going through this experience. Now get the children to lead the procession, as you have planned it. If the procession is able to go outside the worship area of the church for a time, then perhaps you could arrange for the organist or the music group to strike up a triumphant tune when they return.

Song 2

Offering

This may be introduced as a sign of our willingness to trust and follow God.

Offertory prayer

God of life,
we thank you for Jesus who offered his life for the world,
and now offers us new life.
Accept these gifts as tokens that we also offer our lives to you,
trusting you for hope and renewal.
Amen.

Song 3

Reading

Romans 8:11-17 read from a standard Bible. Introduce it with words such as: Paul tells the early Christians that the resurrection of Jesus is able to transform the lives we live here and now. New life, in this world!

Talk (optional)

If you feel it appropriate (and if time permits) point out that while at Easter the principal celebration is of true resurrection, we also celebrate the symbolic value of it – that God leads us through 'death' experiences to new life in the here and now – as, of course, the ancient Hebrews found out at the Red Sea! This is not to make light of the horrible experiences some people have in their lives, or to deny the reality of grief, but simply to hold to the hope that, in the way he knows best, God can lead us through these things.

Prayers of intercession

These could be led entirely by the minister or other adult(s), and/or could include some prayers written by the children themselves – or simply some points that they have raised in discussion.

Song 4

Closing prayer/benediction

Unit 3
Waiting for Pentecost

Overview of the unit

Theme: The Holy Spirit

We take three key events:

Week 1: God gives life to old bones

The story of the valley of dry bones, a traditional Pentecost reading.

Week 2: Ready, steady . . .

Jesus ascends to heaven, telling the disciples to wait for the Holy Spirit to empower them.

Week 3: . . . Go! in the power of the Spirit

The Holy Spirit, symbolised by wind and fire, fills the disciples and empowers them for their mission to the world.

Pentecost all-age worship

This will focus on the Pentecost story – not the dry bones or the Ascension – so the theme of the service will come from Week 3, emphasised in the 'Word and action' material, but some of the art and craft work the children have done in the other weeks will be used to decorate the church and set the wider context of the story.

Week 1: God gives life to old bones

Thinking about it

What's the point?

God gives us life – human beings are more than just a collection of bones, skin and muscles – and our thoughts and feelings are more than the sum of a few electrical impulses. We are *alive* because God has put his own life within us.

Doing it

Prayer

Thank you, loving God,
for giving us life and for wanting us to enjoy it.
Help us this morning to do that by having fun together
and by experiencing your love in the friendships we share.
Amen.

From the known to the unknown

Have handy a mains-powered vacuum cleaner, and try to use it without plugging it in. Hopefully the children will soon put you right. If you want to you can play them along a bit – point out that all the bits are there, all in the right places and connected to one another – so how can plugging into that silly little hole in the wall help?

Of course, human beings are much more than just a collection of bits, aren't we! We've got the life of God within us, and that's the power that makes us really function!

Tell the story: Ezekiel 34:1-14

(See page 68 for a dramatised version of this story.)

This is living!

I'm going to tell you about something really weird that happened to me. I was in a deep valley, and I don't mind telling you it was really creepy – dead quiet, you might say, with not a breath of wind, no birds singing, and just these white bones everywhere – skull bones, toe bones and everything in between, just scattered around all over the place. And dry? You never saw bones as dry as these!

The strange thing was, I didn't know how I'd got there – last thing I could remember, I was lying in a hammock in my garden, with a drink of mango juice in my hand and watching the sunlight make patterns in the leaves of the trees overhead – and the next, I was here. No drink, no nice shady tree and no one for company.

Then I heard a voice – just came from nowhere: 'Hey, man.' I looked all around – nothing. Now, this was seriously scary, and I wanted to go home – but I didn't know which way home was.

The voice came again: 'Hey, man – now don't give me that hard-to-get routine, I know you can hear me. Now, tell me – do you think that these bones can live? Not just walk about, man – I mean *live*? Well, can they? Come on, man, tell it how it is!'

Now, what could I say? I mean, this was seriously weird. Then I decided: either it was God speaking, or I was going mad – and either way there was no use fighting it. Even so, it felt odd talking to a voice that seemed to be inside my head.

'Well?' it said. 'Come on, man, talk to me. D'you reckon these dry bones can have life?'

'God knows!' I answered, feebly.

'Hey, you know something – you're right. I *do* know. And I say *yes*. Now, I'll tell you what you're gonna do now – you're gonna prophesy to these bones – these dry bones – and you're gonna say to them, "O dry bones, hear the word of the Lord!" You got that? Good. Then you're gonna say, "I'm gonna put breath into you and you're gonna live – I mean *Live*, with a big, big, capital L. I'm gonna cover you dry bones up with tissue – and man, I don't mean Kleenex – and I'm gonna give you muscles, and skin, and breathe life into you – and you will live." Have you got that, man? Well, you go tell 'em!'

Well, I'd hardly begun to get the words out when there was such a rattling, and banging, and crashing – I thought all the angels of heaven were playing percussion – and, as I watched, all the bones came together, and they grew tissues, and muscles, and blood vessels, and they got hearts and lungs and all that stuff – I don't mind telling you I was glad when they got their skin on! Then the Voice came back again. By this time I knew who it was all right – only God could have done that.

'Well, man, what d'you think? Good?'

'Oh, very impressive,' I answered, 'but what about all that breath stuff? They don't look very lively to me.'

'That's great, man – you're wising up!' God said. 'Just putting old bones together, that ain't no big deal – and I don't need you to correct my grammar, either, I get enough of that stuff from Gabriel. Now, where was I – oh, yes – but making bones really *live* – man, that's something else. So now you're gonna talk to the wind. Prophesy, man, I say, prophesy! Say, "Come on, you breath, come from the four winds, breathe upon these here dead folk, and let them live." You got that? Go on, man, prophesy!'

Now, we know all about wind in these parts – we get these fierce, hot gales blowing in off the desert – so I braced myself for something impressive. But all I got was this gentle 'whoosh' – I couldn't tell where it came from, or where it was going – really mysterious, it was – and the bodies all got up, thousands of them. God was pretty pleased with himself. 'Hah! Now is that a sight for sore eyes, or is that a sight for sore eyes! Now, my people, the

Israelites – why, they're just like dry bones – little itsy-bitsy bones with no hope or life in them. Now you go and prophesy to them. You tell them I'm going to raise them up. I'm going to give them life, like they've never known before. I'm going to fill them up with my own spirit, and, man, are they going to find out what living is! Now, you go and tell that to my people. You hear? You got me, man? You go tell 'em!'

Respond to the story

Discussion

How do the children think Ezekiel felt as he watched all this happening?

- Impressed?
- Awestruck?
- Nervous?

Why do they think God gave him this vision?

- Just to show off his power?
- To show that there's always hope?
- To show that God can bring new life out of anything?

Song

One or more of the following songs might be used here and/or in the all-age worship:

Be still, for the presence of the Lord
God our Father gave us life
We will praise, we will praise, we will praise the Lord
You've got to move when the Spirit says move

Art and craft

Use the worksheet to cut out and assemble skeletons (this will work best if the worksheet for this week is copied on to white card, rather than just paper).

You might prefer to draw or paint some pictures, either as well or instead. You could include some of Ezekiel standing in the valley of dry bones.

Drama

See the next page for a dramatised version of the story.

Drama: This is living!

(In the narrative version, this story only has two characters. To involve more children, the narrator's part is split, a different child taking Ezekiel's part when he is talking to God. The voice of God could be taken by more than one child in turn – that might be seen as expressing a little of the greatness of God that cannot be portrayed by one person!)

Narrator   I'm going to tell you about something really weird that happened to me. I was in a deep valley, and I don't mind telling you it was really creepy – dead quiet, you might say, with not a breath of wind, no birds singing, and just these white bones everywhere – skull bones, toe bones and everything in between, just scattered around all over the place. And dry? You never saw bones as dry as these! The strange thing was, I didn't know how I'd got there – last thing I could remember, I was lying in a hammock in my garden, with a drink of mango juice in my hand and watching the sunlight make patterns in the leaves of the trees overhead – and the next, I was here. No drink, no nice shady tree and no one for company. Then I heard a voice – just came from nowhere.

God   Hey, man!

Narrator   I looked all around – nothing. Now, this was seriously scary, and I wanted to go home – but I didn't know which way home was.

God   Hey, man – now don't give me that hard-to-get routine, I know you can hear me. Now, tell me – do you think that these bones can live? Not just walk about, man – I mean *live*? Well, can they? Come on, man, tell it how it is!

Narrator   Now, what could I say? I mean, this was seriously weird. Then I decided: either it was God speaking, or I was going mad – and either way there was no use fighting it. Even so, it felt odd talking to a voice that seemed to be inside my head.

God   Well? Come on, man, talk to me. D'you reckon these dry bones can have life?

Ezekiel   God knows!

God   Hey, you know something – you're right. I *do* know. And I say *yes*. Now, I'll tell you what you're gonna do now – you're gonna prophesy to these bones – these dry bones – and you're gonna say to them, 'O dry bones, hear the word of the Lord!' You got that? Good. Then you're gonna say, 'I'm gonna put breath into you and you're gonna live – I mean *Live*, with a big, big, capital L. I'm gonna cover you dry bones up with tissue – and man, I don't mean Kleenex – and I'm gonna give you muscles, and skin, and breathe life into you – and you will live.' Have you got that, man? Well, you go tell 'em!

Narrator   Well, I'd hardly begun to get the words out when there was such a rattling, and banging, and crashing – I thought all the angels of heaven were playing percussion – and, as I watched, all the bones came together, and they grew tissues, and muscles, and blood vessels, and they got hearts and lungs and all that stuff – I don't mind telling you I was glad when they got their skin on! Then the Voice came back again. By this time I knew who it was all right – only God could have done that.

God   Well, man, what d'you think? Good?

Ezekiel   Oh, very impressive, but what about all that breath stuff? They don't look very lively to me.

God   That's great, man – you're wising up! Just putting old bones together, that ain't no big deal – and I don't need you to correct my grammar, either, I get enough of that stuff from Gabriel. Now, where was I – oh, yes – but making bones really *live* – man, that's something else. So now you're gonna talk to the wind. Prophesy, man, I say, prophesy! Say, 'Come on, you breath, come from the four winds, breathe upon these here dead folk, and let them live.' You got that? Go on, man, prophesy!

Narrator   Now, we know all about wind in these parts – we get these fierce, hot gales blowing in off the desert – so I braced myself for something impressive. But all I got was this gentle 'whoosh' – I couldn't tell where it came from, or where it was going – really mysterious, it was – and the bodies all got up, thousands of them. God was pretty pleased with himself.

God   Hah! Now is that a sight for sore eyes, or is that a sight for sore eyes! Now, my people, the Israelites – why, they're just like dry bones – little itsy-bitsy bones with no hope or life in them. Now you go and prophesy to them. You tell them I'm going to raise them up. I'm going to give them life, like they've never known before. I'm going to fill them up with my own spirit, and, man, are they going to find out what living is! Now, you go and tell that to my people. You hear? You got me, man? You go tell 'em!

Can these dry bones live? (Ezekiel 37:3)

Cut these out and assemble them in the right order to make your own skeleton. You can use stud-type paper fasteners for the joints.

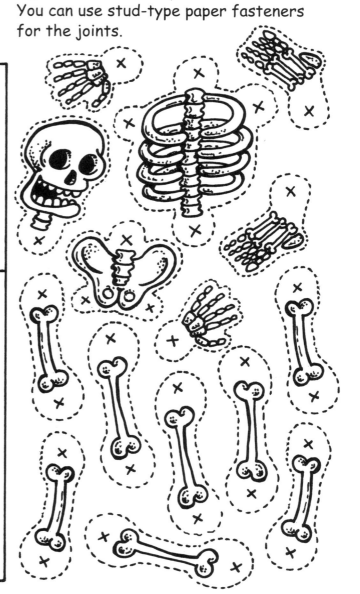

WORDSEARCH

Find the following words in the grid:

DRY BONES, BREATH, WIND, SPIRIT, LIFE, PROPHESY, EZEKIEL, VALLEY, GOD, SKULL, SHIN, ANKLE, FINGER, FOOT, SPINE.

```
E H E K I E T I R I P S
F O T V Y S E H P O R P
I V A A L L E Y S K U I
N A S L E Z E K I E L N
G L K L E R I N G E R E
E L U D R Y B O N E S Z
V E L Y N I B Y R D P E
A Y L F A I L L E Y I K
E T G U D N W I N E R S
F R O O A R K H E A I H
I N G O R A L L E Y T I
L I T E F I N G E R H N
```

Week 2: Ready, steady . . .

Thinking about it

What's the point?

Waiting is not the same as doing nothing – it's about being ready for God's moment when it comes. Sometimes, God calls us to leap into action, but at others he asks us to wait, to watch, to pray, to prepare, so that we're ready when his time is right.

Doing it

Prayer

Loving God,
thank you for time –
not just time to *do* but time to *be*.
Help us to enjoy the time you give us,
to learn and to grow,
so that we're ready to serve you in the best ways
when you decide the time is right.
Amen.

From the known to the unknown

Have the children ever had to be really patient? Perhaps they were bursting to tell someone about a surprise that was planned, but knew they mustn't spoil it. Or, maybe, knowing that they were going to get some money given to them and longing to spend it, have had to wait until it actually arrived. It's very difficult, but sometimes when we're longing to do something we have to wait, because the time isn't quite right yet.

Tell the story: Acts 1

(See page 74 for a dramatised version of this story.)

Wait for it, wait for it . . .

Now, you've heard the stories of Jesus – how he was born, and the things he did, and taught, and all that stuff. And you've heard about how he suffered, and died – and how God raised him up to new life? Right? Well, now I'm going to tell you what happened next.

Of course, the disciples were really glad that Jesus was alive. Well, no, actually, they weren't glad – they were absolutely overjoyed – ecstatic – oh, perhaps you'd better invent your own word, because I don't think there are any in the dictionary that can possibly describe how they felt. Put it this way – if the producers of *Top of the Pops* and *Stars in their Eyes* were fighting over whose show you would star in, you probably wouldn't be one hundredth as happy as the disciples were then.

'Now, don't get carried away,' Jesus told them. 'You're not ready yet to go telling everybody about me – you just wait until the time's right.'

'How're we going to know that?' Peter asked. 'I mean, just how much more right can it be?'

'Oh,' Jesus answered, 'you don't know the half of it! Look, you remember John the Baptist – how he baptised people by pouring water over them and saying they could have a new beginning in their lives? Well, you're in for a baptism, too – but it won't be water poured all over you. Oh, no – it'll be God's Holy Spirit. And if you think you're feeling good now – well, you just wait, that's all.'

'Yeah, yeah, yeah – but when?' James insisted. 'Can't you tell us when you're really going to be the top guy?'

'That's not for you to know' Jesus answered. 'My Father God's got all that sorted. But when the Holy Spirit comes, you'll get the power you need. You're going to tell everyone about me – in Judaea, in Samaria – oh, all over the place, right to the far ends of the earth.'

'That's an awfully long way,' said Peter. 'Will God give me a bigger boat?'

'You worry about that when the time comes,' Jesus smiled. 'Just wait, that's all.'

Peter was about to ask another question, but instead he stopped and stared in amazement. Jesus seemed to be floating – then they all realised that he was leaving them. He was taken up into a big cloud, and they couldn't see him any more. 'Where's he gone?' Peter gasped.

'Oh, where d'you think?' Thomas answered, impatiently. 'He's gone back to his Father, that's where.'

Before they could say any more, they found a couple of strangers had joined them: strange-looking people, all white and shining like something out of a washing powder advert on telly – except that automatic washing powder hadn't been invented then. One of them spoke.

'Hey there, you Galilean dudes! Like, what gives? I mean, what's the scene, man? Why're you standing looking into the sky?'

The disciples looked at one another blankly for a moment, and then the light dawned. 'Angels!' they chorused.

'Gee, man, it takes you guys a long time to catch on!' said the other angel. 'Anyway, just hear this. This Jesus guy, who's just been taken up into heaven, yeah? Well, he's coming back – just like you saw him go, yeah?'

The disciples turned to look at one another again. 'Yeah!' they chorused. A flash made them turn back, and the angels had gone. All that was left was a daisy-chain halo and a hastily scribbled note saying, 'Wait for the power!'

So they went back to Jerusalem and joined Jesus' other friends, including his brothers and his mother, Mary.

'Weird experience, that!' said Peter. ''What are we supposed to do now?'

'What the man said,' said Thomas. 'Wait for the power.'

'That's right,' said Mary. 'I know all about waiting for God – one way or another I've been doing it all my life. He'll move when he's good and ready – just chill, man. Just chill.'

Respond to the story

Discussion

How do the children think the disciples felt about having to wait?

- Excited?
- Frustrated?

How would they cope with that situation?

- Try not to think about it?
- Use the time to get ready?

Song

One or more of the following songs might be used here and/or in the all-age worship:

Jesus isn't dead any more
Jesus, send me the Helper
The King is among us
The Spirit lives to set us free
Wait for the Lord, whose day is near

You might want to use some Easter songs, to remind the children that until Pentecost, we're still in the Easter season.

Art and craft

Draw or paint a picture of Jesus and his friends at his ascension.

This is the key picture, but you might want to do others in addition to it, such as:

- the disciples walking back to Jerusalem
- the disciples waiting together in their meeting room

Drama

See the next page for a dramatised version of the story.

Drama: Wait for it, wait for it . . .

Narrator	Now, you've heard the stories of Jesus – how he was born, and the things he did and taught, and all that stuff. And you've heard about how he suffered, and died – and how God raised him up to new life? Right? Well, now I'm going to tell you what happened next. Of course, the disciples were really glad that Jesus was alive. Well, no, actually, they weren't glad – they were absolutely overjoyed – ecstatic – oh, perhaps you'd better invent your own word, because I don't think there are any in the dictionary that can possibly describe how they felt. Put it this way – if the producers of *Top of the Pops* and *Stars in their Eyes* were fighting over whose show you would star in, you probably wouldn't be one hundredth as happy as the disciples were then. Jesus told them not to get too carried away.
Jesus	You're not ready yet to go telling everybody about me – you just wait until the time's right. Understand, Peter?
Peter	How're we going to know that? I mean, just how much more right can it be?
Jesus	Oh, you don't know the half of it! Look, you remember John the Baptist – how he baptised people by pouring water over them and saying they could have a new beginning in their lives? Well, you're in for a baptism, too – but it won't be water poured all over you. Oh, no – it'll be God's Holy Spirit. And if you think you're feeling good now – well, you just wait, that's all.
James	Yeah, yeah, yeah – but when? Can't you tell us when you're really going to be the top guy?
Jesus	That's not for you to know, James. My Father God's got all that sorted. But when the Holy Spirit comes, you'll get the power you need. You're going to tell everyone about me – in Judaea, in Samaria – oh, all over the place, right to the far ends of the earth.
Peter	That's an awfully long way. Will God give me a bigger boat?
Jesus	You worry about that when the time comes. Just wait, that's all.
Narrator	Peter was about to ask another question, but instead he stopped and stared in amazement. Jesus seemed to be floating – then they all realised that he was leaving them. He was taken up into a big cloud, and they couldn't see him any more.
Peter	Where's he gone?
Thomas	Oh, where d'you think? He's gone back to his Father, that's where.
Narrator	Before they could say any more, they found a couple of strangers had joined them: strange-looking people, all white

and shining like something out of a washing powder advert on telly – except that automatic washing powder hadn't been invented then. One of them spoke.

Angel 1	Hey there, you Galilean dudes! Like, what gives? I mean, what's the scene, man? Why're you standing looking into the sky?
Narrator	The disciples looked at one another blankly for a moment, and then the light dawned.
All disciples together	Angels!
Angel 2	Gee, man, it takes you guys a long time to catch on! Anyway, just hear this. This Jesus guy, who's just been taken up into heaven, yeah? Well, he's coming back – just like you saw him go, yeah?
Narrator	The disciples turned to look at one another again.
All disciples together	Yeah!
Narrator	A flash made them turn back, and the angels had gone. All that was left was a daisy-chain halo and a hastily scribbled note saying, 'Wait for the power!' So they went back to Jerusalem and joined Jesus' other friends, including his brothers and his mother, Mary.
Peter	Weird experience, that! What are we supposed to do now?
Thomas	What the man said – wait for the power. Isn't that right, Mary?
Mary	That's right. I know all about waiting for God – one way or another I've been doing it all my life. He'll move when he's good and ready – just chill, man. Just chill.

You will be my witnesses. (Acts 1:8)

Help Jesus' friends find
their way back to Jerusalem.

WORDSEARCH
Find the following sentence threaded through
the grid:
YOU WILL RECEIVE POWER WHEN THE
HOLY SPIRIT COMES.
You could also find the following words in the grid:
BAPTISED, HOLY SPIRIT, WAIT, ANGELS,
READY, LIFE, TELL.

Crack the code.

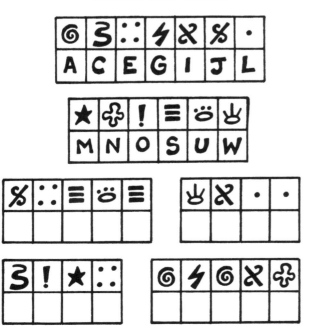

```
R W H E N Z L I F E X T
A E F L E T H E Y Y I I
C D W F K S P D H R H A
L L I O G T A A S O O W
Y W I E P E R N A C L E
O K S B R V R G S O Y Y
U B A P T I S E D M S S
K W H E U E H L L E P I
T H I R G C P S T I I L
E L A L G E R A R L R I
L H C E L R H I A T I P
L S E M O C T S P R T S
```

Week 3: . . . Go! in the power of the Spirit

Thinking about it

What's the point?

God's Holy Spirit gives his people the gifts they need in a particular time and place. For the early disciples, the gift of languages was vital – it enabled them to do God's work. We shouldn't expect that we'll all be given the same gifts, but, in whatever way is best, we believe God will empower us to do his work wherever we are.

Doing it

Prayer

Thank you, loving God,
for all the gifts you give to us –
and especially for the gift of friendship.
Please help us always to remember
that it is truly a gift from your Holy Spirit,
and to help it to grow among us.
Thank you for this time we have,
and may we know that you are here in the love that we share.
Amen.

From the known to the unknown

Can the children remember a time when something suddenly clicked and they found they could do, or understand, something for the first time? That might be a bit what it was like for the disciples in this story.

Tell the story: Acts 2:1-12

(See page 80 for a dramatised version of this story.)

The Spirit comes to those who wait

You know, I never could work out what those people did in my back room. Oh, I'm Zedekiah, by the way, landlord of the Harp and Halo tavern in Jerusalem. Most people just call me Zed – because I snore a lot. Anyway, this bunch of people used to rent one of my rooms every weekend. They seemed a really odd lot to me, I don't mind telling you. Their leader was a man called Peter, and even he didn't seem to know what they were doing, but he had some really weird ideas, I can tell you.

'Well, we're just waiting, that's all,' he said.

'Waiting for what?' I asked.

'We don't know, but we'll know when it happens. Jesus told us to wait.'

Seemed potty to me. Oh, yes, and that was the other thing – this Jesus guy.

Now, we all knew Jesus was dead, see – he'd been publicly executed weeks before, and we'd all watched him die. Well, with no telly we have to get our entertainment somehow. But these friends of his were saying he'd risen from the dead and gone back to heaven to be with God. 'He's going to come back one day,' Peter insisted, 'and we've all got to make sure everyone's ready when he does. That's why we're waiting here – for him to give us the power.'

Well, it seemed to me they were quite capable of telling a tall story without any help from God's office, but they were harmless enough and they paid the rent, so I let them sit in my upstairs room to wait for whatever-it-was – and whenever I had a few spare minutes I'd find an excuse to go and visit them. So there we all were, this one day – Pentecost, it was, which is our harvest festival, and you usually expect people to get a bit carried away then. But this wasn't hysteria, this was real – I was there, and I know. Thomas noticed it first. 'Hey,' he said, 'just listen to that wind.'

He was right – we could hear this roaring, rushing sound just like the big winds that come in off the desert – but it was different.

'Something creepy's happening,' said Philip. 'We can hear the wind, but nothing's being blown around.'

Mary Magdalene joined in. 'I think this is it,' she said. 'I don't know what "it" is, but this is definitely it!'

Women! I ask you! Trouble is, she turned out to be right, but it wasn't over, yet. Suddenly, James started shouting, 'Don't panic! don't panic – the room's on fire!'

Really odd, it was – there seemed to be flames all around us, touching each of the people there, but nothing was burning. And still we could hear that strange wind that no one could actually feel.

Peter flipped completely. 'Yippee!' he yelled, suddenly. 'It's happened! We've got the Power! The power of the Holy Spirit! Let's go tell everybody about Jesus.' And he was gone – just like that. Just like Peter, actually – he never did stop to think.

I tried to talk some sense into them, though. 'You just can't go out there spreading your stories,' I said. 'You need to think, plan, devise a corporate strategy. You've got to identify your consumer base.'

No one was listening. They'd all gone rushing out into the street. Well, I knew they were barking, but I really had to go and see what happened next – so I followed them outside. The first thing I heard was a Cypriot wine merchant talking.

'It's amazing! These are such ordinary people – I mean, they're just so, well, common, really. So how come they can talk to each of us in our own language?'

A Persian carpet-weaver scoffed. 'They're drunk, that's all it is!'

I was just going to tell him that if getting drunk made you fluent in five languages, most of my customers would earn a fortune as interpreters, but Peter got in first.

'Come off it!' he laughed. 'At this time of day? This is God's Spirit, not something out of a bottle – and it's being poured out on the whole world, just as the prophet said it would be.'

Well, there was no holding them after that – soon everyone was hearing about Jesus. Even I ended up believing in him – just don't tell Peter, or I'll never hear the end of it.

Respond to the story

Discussion

Why did the people think the disciples were drunk?

- Because they were so excited?
- Because they were saying that Jesus was alive again?

What did the Holy Spirit actually achieve at that Pentecost?

- Filled the disciples with enthusiasm?
- Broke down barriers between people?
- Helped people understand?

Song

One or more of the following songs might be used here and/or in the all-age worship:

Dance in your Spirit
I, the Lord of sea and sky
I'm enthusiastic
Oh! Oh! Oh! how good is the Lord
Spirit of love
The Spirit lives to set us free

Art and craft

✔ Make a model or picture of the world seen from space. (See 'Word and action' in the All-age worship for how this would be used.) This could be a simple picture, drawn or painted on paper and mounted for display, or it could be a more elaborate three-dimensional model in which case you will need to find a way of standing it securely in the service. Then cut some flames from red and yellow card, not too large but big enough to allow a few words to be written on each one. It might prove easiest to draw these on paper and then photocopy on to card and cut out – you will need enough for each group in the congregation to have a number of cards.

Draw or paint a picture of the disciples with tongues of fire resting on them.

This is the key picture, but you might want to do others in addition to it, such as:

- the disciples waiting in the room
- the disciples in the street arguing with people in the crowd

Drama: The Spirit comes to those who wait

Narrator	You know, I never could work out what those people did in my back room. Oh, I'm Zedekiah, by the way, landlord of the Harp and Halo tavern in Jerusalem. Most people just call me Zed – because I snore a lot. Anyway, this bunch of people used to rent one of my rooms every weekend. They seemed a really odd lot to me, I don't mind telling you. Their leader was a man called Peter, and even he didn't seem to know what they were doing, but he had some really weird ideas, I can tell you.
Peter	Well, we're just waiting, that's all.
Zed	Waiting for what?
Peter	We don't know, but we'll know when it happens. Jesus told us to wait.
Zed	Seemed potty to me. Oh, yes, and that was the other thing – this Jesus guy. Now, we all knew Jesus was dead, see – he'd been publicly executed weeks before, and we'd all watched him die. Well, with no telly we have to get our entertainment somehow. But these friends of his were saying he'd risen from the dead and gone back to heaven to be with God.
Peter	He's going to come back one day, and we've all got to make sure everyone's ready when he does. That's why we're waiting here – for him to give us the power.
Zed	Well, it seemed to me they were quite capable of telling a tall story without any help from God's office, but they were harmless enough and they paid the rent, so I let them sit in my upstairs room to wait for whatever-it-was – and whenever I had a few spare minutes I'd find an excuse to go and visit them. So there we all were, this one day – Pentecost it was, which is our harvest festival, and you usually expect people to get a bit carried away then. But this wasn't hysteria, this was real – I was there, and I know. Thomas noticed it first.
Thomas	Hey, just listen to that wind.
Zed	He was right – we could hear this roaring, rushing sound just like the big winds that come in off the desert – but Philip noticed that it was different.
Philip	Something creepy's happening. We can hear the wind, but nothing's being blown around.
Mary	I think this is it. I don't know what 'it' is, but it's definitely it!
Zed	Women! I ask you! But then, Mary Magdalene had always seemed a bit sus, to me. Trouble is, she turned out to be right, in the end.
James	Don't panic! Don't panic – the room's on fire!
Zed	James was in a right old state – but, to give him his due, it *was* pretty scary. There seemed to be flames all around us, touching each of the people there, but nothing was burning. And still we could hear that strange wind that no one could actually feel. Peter flipped completely.

Peter	Yippee! It's happened! We've got the Power! The power of the Holy Spirit! Let's go tell everybody about Jesus.
Zed	And he was gone – just like that. Just like Peter, actually – he never did stop to think. I tried to talk some sense into them, though. 'You just can't go out there spreading your stories,' I said. 'You need to think, plan, devise a corporate strategy. You've got to identify your consumer base.' But no one was listening. They'd all gone rushing out into the street. Well, I knew they were barking, but I really had to go and see what happened next – so I followed them outside. The first thing I heard was a couple of Cypriot wine merchants talking.
Cypriot 1	It's amazing! These are such ordinary people – I mean, they're just so, well, common, really. So how come they can talk to each of us in our own language?
Cypriot 2	They're drunk, that's all it is!
Zed	I was just going to point out that if getting drunk made you fluent in five languages, most of my customers would earn a fortune as interpreters, but Peter got in first.
Peter	Come off it! At this time of day? This is God's Spirit, not something out of a bottle – and it's being poured out on the whole world just as the prophet said it would be.
Zed	Well, there was no holding them after that – soon everyone was hearing about Jesus. Even I ended up believing in him – just don't tell Peter, or I'll never hear the end of it.

Abound in hope by the power of the Holy Spirit. (Romans 15:13)

These two pictures may look the same
but can you find 10 differences?

WORDSEARCH

Find the following words in the grid:
PENTECOST, HOLY SPIRIT,
POWER, FIRE, WIND,
LANGUAGES, AMAZING,
JESUS, ALIVE, TELL.

```
P E N T E C O S L L E T
J A M A Z I N P O W E E
P E N T E C O S T E N L
P O S E R A M A Z T R S
E G C U Y F I R E W Y E
N W N G S A G F E S C G
T I R I P S Y L O H O A
E N G U Z O W E R I S U
C D Z A M A W E L L D G
S O W E R I M E W O P N
P E N T E C O A R N G A
A L I V E A M A Z I N L
```

Week 4: Pentecost all-age worship

Opening song

A song praising and celebrating the faithfulness of God

Welcome and statement of the theme

Get one or more of the children to point out or hold up the pictures as you sum up the story:

In Junior Church during the past few weeks, we've been learning about the Holy Spirit. We started with the story of Ezekiel's vision of dry bones in the Old Testament, where God not only put the dry bones together, but breathed life into them. The Hebrew word for 'wind' or 'breath' is the same as the one used for the Holy Spirit, and God said to Ezekiel that he was going to put his breath – his Spirit – into his people. Then we read about the ascension of Jesus into heaven, after his resurrection, when he told his disciples to wait for the coming of the Holy Spirit to empower them – and how the disciples obeyed Jesus by waiting in Jerusalem until the time was right. Then, finally, we read the story of the gift of the Holy Spirit at Pentecost, which drove the waiting disciples out into the world to spread the Good News. This is what we're celebrating today, of course. We'll take that a little further in a few moments.

Prayer

Lord God,
we thank you for the gift of your Holy Spirit
to encourage and empower your people.
We pray that today you will lift our worship,
fill us with joy and hope,
and inspire us to spread your gospel.
Through Jesus Christ, our Lord.
Amen.

Word and action

Have the story read, in either dramatised or narrative form, and then divide the congregation into groups, giving a few cards to each group. They are going to put together a prayer list to set the world on fire! Ask them to discuss and write on the flames the gifts they would pray that the Holy Spirit will give to this church, to empower its mission, thinking of local issues as well as wider concerns. Assure them that their efforts will be taken seriously, and the cards later used to compile (or complement) a prayer calendar for the church. Examples might be: the gift of working with young people; the gift of encouragement to sustain people going through hard times; the gift of computer skills to enable the church to set up its own website; the gift of hospitality to welcome newcomers to the area – and so on. Have a few such examples ready in case they need help, but don't jump the gun – you might get even better ideas from the groups if you don't steer them!

After a few minutes, call them back to order and ask what they have come up with. Let people come forward and, using Blue-tack or whatever is suitable, stick the flames to the world picture or model. Remind the congregation how these cards are going to be used, and then end the session with a short prayer for grace to wait expectantly.

Song 2

Offering

This may be introduced as symbolising the gifts the church already has which are being offered to God for renewal in his service.

Offertory prayer

Holy Spirit of God,
inspire and inflame your church here,
that the gifts we offer and the gifts we hope to receive
may be used for the spreading of God's kingdom.
Through Jesus Christ our Lord.
Amen.

Song 3

Reading

1 Corinthians 12:27-13:7 read from a standard Bible. Introduce it with words such as: Paul tells us which, of all the gifts of the Holy Spirit, is the most important.

Talk (optional)

If you feel it appropriate (and if time permits) you could simply emphasise the point that the gifts God gives us are not for us to glorify ourselves, but to show his love to others and thus glorify him. One often hears the gifts talked about in very self-indulgent ways as if they were given to the church for its own benefit. But if love is the greatest gift, there must be a little more to it than that, mustn't there?

Prayers of intercession

These could be led entirely by the minister or other adult(s), and/or could include some prayers written by the children themselves – or simply some points that they have raised in discussion.

Song 4

Closing Prayer/Benediction